LAST CALL
at the
7-ELEVEN

by Kevin Cowherd

Fine Dining at 2 A.M.,

The Search for Spandex People,

and Other Reasons to Go On Living

The Bancroft Press
Baltimore, MD

ISBN 0-9635376-3-6
Library of Congress Catalogue Number
Printed in the United States of America

Designed by Melinda Russell Design, Baltimore, Maryland
Composed in Electra by Melinda Russell Design
and the Bancroft Press

Dedication

To Nancy, who always laughs, and to Sean, Chrissie and Jamie.

Acknowledgments

Let me say this about acknowledgments: Most of 'em will put you to sleep faster than an axe handle upside the head.

But the ones in this book are different. In a number of test markets, people who read these acknowledgments actually reported increased energy levels, a heightened sense of well-being, and an improved sex life. So if you blow off these next seven or eight paragraphs, it's no skin off *my* nose, believe me.

Thanks to Bruce Bortz, who first envisioned this book, awoke in a cold sweat, and *still* decided to go through with the project. This is a brave man — not to mention the best publisher a guy could ask for.

Thanks to Jack Lemmon, who gave an unknown humor writer his start, and to Mike Davis, who gave that same humor writer more freedom than he deserved. I bet they both feel like Dr. Frankenstein now.

Thanks to Steve Proctor, who believed in the column and gave it a new life, and to Rob Hiaasen, who helped decide the title by saying: "Well, that one's not as stupid as the last one …"

Thanks to Bob Bonney. Like Ali, he was The Greatest.

Thanks to Abe Bortz and David Bortz, who sifted through more than 1,200 columns for this book and never *once* went out and stabbed anyone — at least to my knowledge. Thanks, too, to Andrew Bortz, computer guru extraordinaire, for his incredible kindness and patience in dealing with the technology-impaired.

Thanks especially to my mother, Noreen Cowherd; my sister, Maura Rose; my brother, Steve Cowherd, and their families for all their love and support. And to Dorothy Phelan, Beth and Doug Diesu and their kids, and Susan Scully for the same reasons.

If I left anyone out, you know I didn't mean it.

I've just had a lot on my mind lately.

Contents

The Non-Renaissance Man

O.D.ing on Holidays

Get Your Motor Runnin'

The Love Thing

Introduction

For some reason, people seem to focus on my name a lot, especially at cocktail parties.

It's a rather … *unusual* name, isn't it?" someone will say, sipping a Heineken and studying me intently.

"Kevin?" I say. "I don't think so. Hell, I must know a half-dozen Kevins myself, not to mention my nephew Kevin in … "

"No, not *Kevin*," this person replies, and now there's a hint of something else in his voice — wariness, perhaps — as if he's suddenly determined that the person he's speaking to is either a bit slow or possibly even disturbed. "Your, um, *other* name."

"Oh. You mean Cowherd?" I say.

At this point, I rake another Ritz cracker through the onion dip and stare at it thoughtfully. Then my shoulders begin to shake, almost imperceptibly at first, and then I dissolve into a series of great, heaving sobs, until finally the poor bastard with the Heineken says: "Look, I didn't mean to … the bar's over that way, isn't it?"

So, don't ask me about my name, OK? It's English-Irish, dates back hundreds of years to some people who, I don't know, were into cows. That's all you have to know.

Touchy? You betcha. *You* try going through life with the name Cowherd. See if *you're* skipping down the sidewalk singing "Zippity-Doo-Dah."

Now that we've got the last name out of the way, let me tell you a little about myself. I'm 43, married, with three kids. I live in the suburbs of Baltimore, which means I give directions to my house that include such historic landmarks as Mr. Tire and International House of Pancakes.

I grew up in a small town in New York and hate cities, so if I have to pass Bob's House O' Lamps five times a day and see some jerk dressed in a smiley-face light bulb costume waving at traffic, that's fine with me.

As you may or may not be able to tell, this book is a collection of columns. I wrote most of them for the Baltimore *Sun* and *Evening Sun.* The latter died a few months ago and was quickly zipped into the body bag of afternoon newspapers in America.

These pieces are all supposed to be funny, but I'll leave it up to you as to whether they really are or not.

On second thought, don't tell me if they're *not* funny, because I'm not sure I could handle that. See, the humor columnist faces enough rejection in everyday life without hearing from people who don't think his *books* are funny.

Out in public, the humor columnist will often encounter a reader who recognizes him from his just-out-of-San Quentin mug shot in the paper and who says: "God, that was a funny piece you wrote the other day! The one about ... what was it about again?"

"The Health Gestapo?" replies the humorist, trying to be helpful.

"No, *that* one was stupid."

"Dental hygienists? How they're always on you about flossing and ...."

"No, I didn't like that one at all."

"Thanksgiving dinner with Howard Stern?"

"No. Hmmm, maybe it was somebody *else's* column."

At this point, the humor columnist, wearing a thin, frozen smile, will likely excuse himself, make his way to his car and drive home slowly.

Once there, he'll go down to the basement, set his rocking chair a foot or two from the cold, cinder-block wall, and sit there rocking and rocking in the dark for many hours, trying to figure out where it all went wrong.

Now maybe you're thinking: Fine, fine, you got a tough life, pal. But what's with the stupid title for the book?

The truth is, I hang out in 7-Elevens a lot. And let me tell you: there's no more fascinating a place to be at 2 in the morning.

I've seen secretaries, giddy from three margaritas, experience hours of fun with the "Test Your Blood Pressure" machine. I've seen construction workers with bloodshot eyes read aloud from the ingredients listed on a Hostess fruit pie like it was Act One of "Othello." I've seen frat boys in polo shirts wolf down foot-long Slim Jims in two bites while thumbing through the latest edition of *Biker Girl*.

People talk about the lack of quality entertainment nowadays. All I can say is: go visit a convenience store when the bars let out. It makes cable look like stamp collecting.

Anyway, I wrote a column about an early-morning run to the 7-Eleven. And it's in here somewhere. And that's how we came up with the book's stupid title.

So let's not hear any more whining about this. After all, I don't remember any helpful ideas from *you* about what to call this book.

Rich, Famous, and Dead

Larry King's greatest coup

Breezy opening theme. Fade to TV studio. Close-up of Larry King at his desk. He's wearing a blue shirt, red polka-dot tie and trademark suspenders. Across from him is a bearded figure dressed in flowing robes. His face is bathed in shimmering light.

LK: "Well, we got Him! It wasn't easy. We've been negotiating with His people for some time now. There've been some big names on this show lately: Ross Perot, Ivana Trump, Magic Johnson. But none bigger than my next guest, adored and worshipped by millions around the world. Please welcome... God!"

GOD: "Thanks, Larry. Nice to be here."

LK: "You were telling me at lunch today... this is not the Second Coming as called for in the *Book of Revelation?*"

GOD: "That's right, Larry. This is strictly a spur-of-the moment visit. The world's going through a tough time right now. I thought this might help."

LK: "I imagine it's been an adjustment."

GOD: "Well, I've been asked to do some photo ops, tighten the parables for sound bites, that sort of thing. Plus we're doing 'Arsenio' next week, too. That should be something."

LK: "Let's go right to the phones. Sacramento, California, hello."

CALLER: "Hi, Larry? Great show."

LK: "Thanks."

CALLER: "God?"

GOD: "Yes, my son."

CALLER: "I'm a big admirer of Yours, but how do you explain Geraldo?"

GOD: "My thinking was: intelligent, aggressive reporter, ethnic good looks — can't miss. Looking back on it now, I didn't think he'd be nearly so annoying. But hindsight is always 20/20."

LK: "Kalamazoo, Michigan."

CALLER: "Larry, enjoyed your show with Roxanne Pulitzer the other night."

LK: "Your question for God, please."

CALLER: "Yes, I'm curious as to how the eternal struggle against Satan is going."

5

GOD: "We've had some recent setbacks — Pol Pot comes immediately to mind. And crack cocaine. But I like to think we're winning."

LK: "Tell us about your new book."

GOD: "It's called *Bright Lights, Holy City: My Life Story*. It's sort of an updated version of the Old and New Testaments. Michael J. Fox wrote the introduction. It's got easier-to-read print, enhanced graphics, lots of pictures."

LK: "So it deals with ... "

GOD: "See, when we first pitched a book, Random House said: 'The Creation, Adam and Eve, the Great Flood, Sodom and Gomorrah... it's all been done. Put some new stuff in there.' So this is basically a what's-He-doing-now? book."

LK: "And the book tour starts ... ?"

GOD: "We're in New York Friday and Saturday, and Boston Sunday. Let's see, Philly on the 19th... you'd think my memory would be better... back to Washington on the 20th. Atlanta after that."

LK: "Someone told me Paramount has an option to..."

(Suddenly there is a disturbance off-camera. Camera pans to distraught woman with tears streaming down her face attempting to rush set. She is restrained by security guards.)

LK: *(Visibly upset)* "For God's sake!"

GOD: "No problem, I get that a lot."

LK: "Fort Worth, Texas, for God."

CALLER: "Yes, how do You answer the skeptics who say: 'If He's really God, how come He had to rest on the seventh day after creating heaven and earth?'"

LK: "Good question."

GOD: "Very good question. All I can say is — and I don't want this to sound obtuse — that was the game plan."

LK: "Honolulu, Hawaii."

CALLER: "In the Book of Deuteronomy, You said that..."

GOD: *(Irritated)* "Please! I *know* what I said. Let's just get on with... sorry. It's been a long day. I was up at 6:00 doing the 'Today Show.'"

LK: "I gotta ask you... you did a video?"

GOD: "Well, I wanted to get my message across without hurling lightning bolts or drying up rivers, etc. So, I thought a video... it's like those 'Be Cool, Stay in School' public service spots, only we're talking about Eternal Salvation. I did it with Van Halen."

LK: "My secretary Helen wants to know if you've performed any miracles lately."

GOD: *(Chuckling)* "I'm thinking of having Chevy Chase win an Oscar for Best Actor."

LK: "Well, it's not like making the Nile run blood-red, but..."

GOD: "Maybe we'll make the Amtrak trains run on time."

LK: "My guest has been God. The book is: *Bright Lights, Holy City: My Life Story*. Can't thank you enough for being here."

GOD: "My pleasure, Larry."

(The two shake hands. Larry teases upcoming CNN news. Fade to black.)

Barbara Walters:
Two perspectives

The whole thing started over Barbara Walters, which is a silly damn thing to fight over, but there you have it.

What happened was, Nancy was reading a magazine profile on Barbara Walters, one of those long-winded puff jobs wherein the subject is portrayed as the logical successor to St. Francis of Assisi in terms of warmth, compassion, and contributions to humanity.

Just to get the conversation rolling, I said: "A Barbara Walters piece. Boy, *there's* a lot of trees that died for nothing."

Well. You know how you'll say something and, even as the words are leaving your mouth, you know it's the wrong thing to say?

This was the wrong thing to say.

"You have a problem with Barbara Walters?" she said.

"I have a lot of problems with Barbara Walters," I said.

"You have a lot of problems, period," she said.

"Barbara Walters is smarmy, maudlin, egotistical..."

"Are you through?" she said.

"And that sickening oh-so-earnest look she fixes on people, God! I have to leave the room when I see that."

"Why don't you leave the room now?"

Nine-thirty at night and we're fighting about Barbara Walters. Apparently there was nothing on TV.

"Here's what *really* gets me," I said. "Your buddy Barbara will be interviewing someone like, oh, Stallone, OK? But instead of asking him something normal, like how many guys will Rocky beat the crap out of in his next movie, she'll furrow her brow and look at him with those big cow eyes and say: 'Sly, do you think the Far Eastern religions are on to something with this emphasis on a middle course between mortification and the pursuit of ambition?' And Stallone will look at her like: 'Wha-a-a?'"

"Stallone is a jerk," said my wife.

"OK. Fine. But what kind of stupid question is that? Even if you're interviewing someone like Jeanne Kirkpatrick, it's *still* a stupid question."

"Maybe she just..."

"Or Roseanne Barr," I said. "Or Arnold. Or whatever her name is now. She'll be sitting there scratching herself or playing footsie with her husband — you want to talk about a *jerk* — and Barbara will ask her something about the Balkanization of our society, how we seem to be increasingly fragmented and... I mean, this is Roseanne Arnold, not Henry Kissinger."

"Barbara Walters is the best interviewer in the business," said my wife.

"The best in the business?! Let me say two little words, OK? Mike Wallace. And Mike Wallace isn't going to sit down with Yasser Arafat in some sun-dappled villa in Tunis and look deeply into the man's eyes and say: 'Yasser, if you were a tree, what kind of tree would you be?'"

"Barbara Walters never said that," Nancy said. "That was something the media..."

"Oh, here we go with the media," I said.

"...blew completely out of proportion. Look, I don't want to talk about it anymore."

For a moment, silence descended upon the room. She pretended to go back to her reading. But I knew she still wanted to talk about it. Thirteen years of marriage, you can tell when a person wants to talk about something.

"Hugh Downs has carried '20/20' for years," I said quietly.

"HUGH DOWNS?!" She looked at me like I said Doogie Howser.

"The man is a rock," I said. "Solid, dependable. A real pro."

"Hugh Downs is boring."

"Only boring people would find Hugh Downs boring."

"He looks so ill-at-ease," my wife said.

"I'd be ill-at-ease, too, with Barbara across from me. I'd be afraid we'd be in the middle of some big story on, oh, lead pollutants, and she'd ask me what my favorite color was."

"I'm sure Barbara would be delighted to hear the flattering things you're..."

"Listen," I said, "you think Barbara Walters cares what some hack writer from Baltimore thinks? She's a big-shot. Fabulously wealthy, powerful. A jet-setter. Someone hands her a critical column at dinner, she just yawns and turns to one of the servants and says: 'James, throw another five lobsters in the pot.'"

"I don't want to talk about it anymore," she said.

"Fine with me," I said.
I'm glad we got *that* settled.

Next Donahue: Death, live

Phil Donahue says he would broadcast an execution on his talk show. "What's wrong with it?" he said. "Let's see future bad guys watch these people fry right here on television."
— *Associated Press*

(Breezy opening theme. Fade in to studio audience applauding. Donahue is standing stage left next to an ominous-looking electric chair. He wears a bemused expression.)

Donahue: "Thank you, thank you. Well, we've got a special treat for you today. Billy Clyde Semple has been on Death Row in Florida's Railford Prison since 1987. He was convicted of killing three people in a bizarre murder-for-hire plot that unraveled when — get this — the getaway driver fell asleep at the wheel! What is this — 'The Gang That Couldn't Shoot Straight?'"

(Laughter.)

Donahue: "But now he's exhausted his appeals, so we're gonna put him to death right here on our show!"

(Wild applause.)

Donahue: "With me are Railford Assistant Warden Earl McFarland and the executioner, who must by law remain anonymous behind this smoked glass partition. Mr. McFarland, nice to see you, sir."

McFarland: "Nice to be here, Phil."

Donahue: "Now meet Billy Clyde Semple. An eighth-grade dropout, Mr. Semple joined the Army at age 17, but was thrown out for slugging his commanding officer. He drifted through a series of menial jobs until that fateful morning when... yes, Mr. Semple?"

Semple: "I didn't do it."

Donahue *(cups hands to ear)*: "Come again?"

Semple: "I... didn't do it."

Donahue *(rolls eyes)*: "Oh, come *on*, Billy Clyde! Pul-leeze!"

(Boos and hisses.)

Donahue *(looks beseechingly at audience)*: "Doesn't *every* Death Row con say he didn't do it? I mean... yes, ma'am. You have a question?"

(Phil scurries over with outstretched microphone to a middle-aged woman wearing a T-shirt that says: "Let Me Throw the Switch!")

Audience member: "Yes, I'd like to ask Mr. Semple if he feels any remorse for the families of the men he murdered."

Donahue: "Billy Clyde?"

Semple: "Look, I didn't do it! A bunch of us were drinking that day. Then someone suggested we take a ride to..."

Donahue: "By the way, don't forget that on tomorrow's show, our topic will be: School principals by day, drag queens at night. I'm sorry, Billy Clyde. You were saying...?"

Semple: "Uh, so we went to the convenience store to buy more beer. And when we got there, all three guys were already dead! I had nothing to do with it!"

Donahue *(hands on hips)*: "You know what gets me? You know what really burns my bacon? You come here with your pious baloney, all your neat, pat little answers. YOU JUST DON'T WANT TO FRY, DO YOU?"

Semple *(agitated)*: "Phil, there were *no* fingerprints at the scene and *no* eyewitnesses! Plus it was a known fact that the district attorney and presiding judge were..."

Donahue: "I'm sorry, we have to break for a commercial. We'll be right back."

(Applause. Fade out.)

(Two-minute commercial break.)

(Fade in.)

Donahue: "Let me give you the lineup for next week's shows. On Monday, Joey Buttafuoco joins us; now he says Amy Fisher was his weekly bridge partner, that's all. Tuesday: Real Fat People — The Fattest You've Ever Seen! Wednesday: Nazi lesbians on college campuses. Thursday we'll talk with ex-'Star Trek' cast member and current cult de-programmer George Takei. Friday: The Rat Lady from Madagascar. Caller, you have a question?"

Caller: "Yes, I'd like to know how many volts Mr. Semple will be receiving?"

Donahue: "Mr. McFarland?"

McFarland: "Approximately 2,000."

Donahue: "Two thousand volts! What is this — a junior varsity execution?!"

(Laughter.)

Donahue: "Anyway, we're almost out of time. Mr. McFarland, if you'll do the honors..."

(Semple is led by guards to the electric chair. Electrodes are fastened to the shaved portions of his head, arms and legs. The guards step back. A gentle wisp of smoke is visible. Semple seems to stiffen for an instant, then slumps forward.)

Donahue: "Well, that about does it. The coroner'll be out in a moment to verify that Billy Clyde is, in fact, dead. Remember: Joey Buttafuoco on Monday. So long, everyone."

(Applause. Closing theme.)

(Fade to black.)

A veritable feast of personalities

Thanksgiving dinner with:

HOWARD STERN: "Yo, sweetie, pass the cranberry sauce. What's your name? Laurie? Yeah, lemme ask you something, Laurie: Are you stupid? Because only a real friggin' moron would pass the mashed potatoes when I asked for the friggin' cran... holy geez, who's the babe at the end of the table? Will ya look at the pumpkins on her! Who is that? Is that my sister-in-law Andrea? Yo, Andrea! Nice (BLEEPS)!"

(Everyone at the table groans.) "What? I say something wrong? No, really, tell me! What, you can't say (BLEEPS)?! It's not like I said (BLEEPS), right?"

(More groans.) "What is it with you people? I thought the Puritans died 300 years ago. Robin, someone called me a misogynist today. You believe that? So I smacked her!"

(Groans.) "What?! What'd I say *now*? Sweetie, the cranberry sauce. Today, all right?"

DAVID LETTERMAN: "Ohh-kay. Let's see... the mayor of Baltimore, Kurt Schmoke, ladies and gentleman. SCHHHMOKE! I don't have a joke here... just love saying that name. SCHHH-MOKE!

"Let's see... what're we doing next? Gravy, I guess. Gravy on the mashed potatoes. Do we have time for this? Paul?"

(Paul swallows a forkful of dressing, smiles and points at Dave. Dave fires a pea at him with his knife.)

"Ladies and gentlemen, this is comedy. Yeah, this is what CBS is paying the big bucks for. Joining us later for mince pie... Teri Garr, Martin Mull, and comedian Rick Martinez.

"Did I tell you I got another speeding ticket, Paul? Yeah, 80 in a 55. And that woman's back. In my house... yeah, that one, the nut. Saw her upstairs a few minutes ago. Must've broken in through the skylight.

"Good God, she's rappelling into my home now! Do we have any rappelling music, Paul?"

(Paul puts down a huge drumstick, reaches one arm over chair, plays a polka riff on the synthesizer.)

"Mmmmm, this gravy is delicious! What else? I see President Clinton is..."

BARBARA WALTERS: "Burt, forgive me, but I must ask you: What was it like living with Loni in those terrible months? Pass the biscuits, please. You seem so... bitter. Is that the margarine? Yes, please, I'll take some.

"Burt, did you ever want to be anything besides a movie star? Like... I don't know, some sort of bird? A turkey, maybe? Did Loni ever want to be a turkey?

"I interviewed Saddam Hussein once and he said he wanted to be a dove. Did you ever want to be a dove, Burt? Did Loni ever want to be a dove? Are those creamed onions? Yes, please, just a few.

"Somebody once told me — it was either Hugh Downs or Arnold Schwarzenegger — that he wanted to be an Arctic tern. Did you ever want to be an Arctic tern, Burt? Did Loni ever...?"

ROSS PEROT: "Right away, I see us havin' a real problem here. Are you gonna let me talk? Huh? Is that possible? Thank yew. Now, as I was sayin', would you like some white meat or some of that...

"So, am I gonna be able to finish a sentence? Just one sentence? You know who you remind me of? That turniphead Gore. You're not with the media, are you?

"How 'bout some broccoli? You're gonna love this broccoli, it's from right here in... what was that? Thought I heard something outside the window. Sergeant Muldauer, take a platoon of your SWAT boys and see if any of them *Eye*-ranian fundamentalists are sneakin' around. Castro sent some people to kill me, too, y'know.

"How 'bout some sweet potatoes? These here are from... son, is this how it's gonna be? You inneruptin' me all the time?"

JERRY LEWIS: "Everybody know each other? No? OK, before we dig in, let me handle the introductions.

"Immediately to my right, the giant who's been with me since we started these gatherings, maybe the biggest heart in Hollywood, Mr. Ed McMahon!"

(Ed nods, says: "Hiyo.")

"This next lady is class all the way and helps define what this business is all about: Miss Linda Lavin!

"To her right... what can you say about this next gentleman?" *(Jerry's eyes moisten.)* "A super individual and a super talent, a man who's always there for me, Mr. Robert Goulet!

"God rest his soul, but when Sammy was alive, he used to say of our next guest: 'Jerry, the cat is Numero Uno.' And indeed he is. A unique talent and my main man in the radio industry: Mr. Casey Kasem!

"Over there, next to the stuffing, a marvelous performer..."

Dr. Jack: a painkiller for all occasions

If Dr. Jack Kevorkian wrote an advice column:

Dear Dr. Kevorkian,
"Melanie" and I were best friends throughout high school and
college and shared many wonderful moments. She is getting married in
a few months. Yesterday I found out that she asked "Lisa" to be her
maid of honor. I am hurt and embarrassed. Should I just swallow my
pride and attend the wedding and pretend that everything is alright?
— Rita L., San Antonio, Texas

Dr. Kevorkian responds: My dear woman, what you are
enduring is the unendurable. Dr. Jack read your letter and within
seconds was reduced to great, wracking sobs. The room grew cold. A
thick, dark cloud of gloom and despair descended over me.

Fortunately, there is a way "out" of your misery. Do you have
access to an automobile and a garage with poor ventilation? Legal
technicalities in your state prevent me from being more forthcoming.
Soak some towels and place them over any structural openings to
prevent fumes from escaping.

God speed on your sweet journey.

Dr. Kevorkian,
I am 19-years-old and so is my boyfriend "Freddy." At a fraternity
party last week, I found him all over this bimbo, kissing and groping
her. This is the third time I've caught him with someone else. He says
he loves me, but I'm not so sure. Your opinion please. — Martha M.,
Baltimore

Dr. Kevorkian responds: When Dr. Jack was your age, he too was
involved in an unfortunate affair of the heart. Sylvia was the little
tramp's name. It turned out she was "seeing" a muscular linebacker
on the football team while Dr. Jack diligently studied night after night
for his pre-med courses.

Obviously there was only one thing to do. Slipping into the
gymnasium boiler room one night, I tied a length of rope to one of
the ceiling pipes, fashioned a noose with the other end, and climbed
up on a chair.

Unfortunately, the rope was made from an inferior hemp and broke soonafter I jumped. When I came to, instead of finding myself in the arms of a loving angel, I was being shaken by a frightened janitor with garlic breath.

Now for the good news: The rope made today is much sturdier. And there are exposed ceiling pipes everywhere.

I envy you. You go to a place of eternal Light and Peace.

Dear Dr. Kevorkian,

At a recent cocktail party, my husband "Sol" insisted the toilet paper in one's bathroom should unroll from the top. I said it's just the opposite. Several friends agreed with me. Who's right? — Ellen L. Lewiston, N.Y.

Dr. Kevorkian responds: My God, woman, how do you stand it? A bitter, tyrannical husband who micro-manages your life, virulently anti-Semitic friends, days of unrelieved monotony broken only by scatological discussions conducted through a numbing, alcoholic haze.

I see you live near Niagara Falls. There is a secluded bluff unpatrolled by park rangers on the east side of the gorge. The elevation is nearly 200 feet. In a matter of seconds, your pain would be over.

Farewell. I look forward to our meeting one day in the Great Beyond.

Dear Dr. Kevorkian,

Your reply to the 33-year-old record company executive who struck out three times (twice with the bases loaded) in a rec league softball game was way out of line.

You suggested emptying the contents of 60 Seconol tablets into a small bowl of applesauce and then eating the combination. Yet you neglected to mention that a couple of belts of vodka would cause the drugs to be absorbed that much more quickly into the bloodstream. Come on, Doc, you're slipping! — Dave W., Los Angeles

Dr. Kevorkian responds: You're right, Dave, it was a bad day for Dr. Jack. I was gripped by a suffocating depression and laid out by several grand-mal seizures that left me sweat-soaked and disoriented.

In addition, a noise like a high-speed drill — *EEEE! EEEE!* — filled my head as well as horrible visions of hyenas with bloody mouths ripping my flesh.

My best to you and your family.

(<u>Note</u>: *Due to the volume of mail, Dr. Kevorkian regrets that he cannot personally appear at the door of each and every person who writes in.*)

At least Warren Beatty keeps his mouth shut

One problem with this country is that nobody can keep a secret any more, and if you don't believe me, just ask Warren Beatty.

If you can get him to even *talk* about this. Personally, I think he might slam the door in your face and sic the Dobermans on you no matter how delicately the subject is broached. Which I could certainly understand. Because if there is anyone who deserves to be ticked off about people who can't keep secrets, it's Warren Beatty.

Tell you what I mean. Here is Warren Beatty, right? Big Hollywood star. Successful. Famous. Incredibly good looking. The lead in the summer's hottest new movie, "Dick Tracy," who stands to make $900 million or whatever, not that he was clipping Kentucky Fried Chicken coupons before this.

Yet at a time in his life when he should be rolling along, singing a song, people are revealing the most intimate details of the man's life. Joan Collins, for one.

I'm reading a profile on Warren Beatty the other day and suddenly here's this quote from Joan Collins: "He was insatiable. Three, four, five times a day... and he was able to accept telephone calls at the same time."

Mother of God. Now, I don't presume to speak for Warren Beatty. But it seems to me that this "insatiable" stuff is not the kind of info you want to get around, certainly nothing you'd want Mom to read back home in Dubuque or wherever.

At least I wouldn't want my mom to read it about *me*. Even if I *were* insatiable. (Which I'm not saying I am. Nor am I denying it. I'm just saying... let's drop the whole thing, OK?)

The point is, it seems to me the issue of Warren Beatty's satiability, or lack of same, should remain between Mr. Beatty and Ms. Collins (or Warren and Joan). It should not be bandied about in the media for cheap public titillation.

Same thing with this business of Warren Beatty taking phone calls during sex. On the face of it, sure, this sounds impressive. Me, I can barely remember to breathe during sex, never mind carry on a decent telephone conversation. Not that I should be telling you all this. It's just that... never mind.

But if one *were* able to converse gracefully over the phone while entwined in various positions espoused by the Kama Sutra, I don't see how that's anyone else's business.

Except the entwin-ee. And the entwin-or. Which in this case would be Mr. Beatty and Ms. Collins. Warren and Joan. War and Jo. You know who I mean.

Again, the point is that if you're Joan Collins, I don't see why you have to blab all over town about Warren Beatty's ability to simultaneously make love and close a three-picture deal with Universal Studios on the horn.

Please. Is nothing sacred?

On the other hand, Warren Beatty himself seems to be the kind of guy who can keep a secret.

The man has made love to some of the most beautiful and famous women in the world, right? But you never hear of him elbowing, say, Jack Nicholson and remarking: "Hey, Jack, I ever tell you about Julie Christie? When she gets really excited in bed, she makes these little high-pitched squeals, sorta like "EEE-III-EEE! It's funnier than hell. Sounds like a damn dolphin or something."

No. Warren Beatty doesn't talk out of school. About Julie Christie. Or anyone else, for that matter. Even to Jack Nicholson. And if ever there was a guy who would appreciate that sort of frank, earthy discussion, it would be Jack Nicholson. (Not that I ever met the man. But you hear things.)

Getting back to Warren Beatty, however, say what you will about him, but the man is discreet.

I have yet to read an interview with him where he's quoted as saying that Diane Keaton liked to recite whole passages from the childhood nursery rhyme "I'm a Little Teapot" while making love.

And I have yet to see an "Entertainment Tonight" piece where he reveals that, sure, sex with Leslie Caron was great — except when she insisted that the two of them spray themselves with Lemon Pledge (with the new improved anti-streaking formula) before hitting the bedroom.

No. Warren Beatty knows how to keep his mouth shut. I'll bet he could reveal some things about Madonna and those torpedo brassieres that would make your hair curl.

Or *my* hair curl, anyway.

Dear Leonard Nimoy:
You can't sing, so don't sing

Let me begin by saying that singing is a right accorded to each of us by the U.S. Constitution, or if it isn't, it should be.

Unfortunately, too many of us abuse this right. Let's be blunt here. Too many of us lift our voices in song when it would be far better for everyone concerned if we just hummed along, or perhaps shut up entirely.

In our desire to sing even something simple, say, for instance, the chorus of "Help Me Rhonda," many of us produce a sound eerily similar to the bleating of a farm animal.

By the way, I count myself among those poor unfortunates whom humorist Roy S. Blount describes as the "singing impaired."

My singing is best left in the shower, where it can mercifully be drowned out by the roar of water, and therefore is not a threat to frighten small children.

But at least I admit I'm a lousy singer. I don't try to pretend I can carry a tune, like certain other people, who shall remain nameless... Even though they're in show business. And they think they're so much better than everyone else. And they can't sing a lick.

Oh, what the hell. Leonard Nimoy, for instance.

Many of you will remember Nimoy as the competent if somewhat wooden actor who portrayed pointy-eared, pain-in-the-neck Dr. Spock in the "Star Trek" series.

Anyway, Nimoy made a pretty good living for himself off "Star Trek," even though it was universally assumed that an attentive filing cabinet could have brought the same amount of interpretation to the role.

In any event, the poor man apparently experienced some sort of psychotic episode some years back, as he awoke one morning thinking: By God, I can sing, I will cut an album.

Unfortunately, neither Mrs. Nimoy nor any other family members were around to wrestle him to the ground and slap some sense into him.

So the man was actually allowed to venture past the security guards and into a recording studio, where he cut — you should pardon the expression — an album.

Let me tell you about this album, if you never, um, experience it for yourself.

It was the worst album ever recorded in the history of the music industry. No, that's not strong enough. It was the worst collection of *sound* ever heard since the dawn of civilization.

To this day, if you mention Nimoy's album to someone like, say, Aretha Franklin, the poor woman is likely to clutch her chest and begin hyperventilating.

Maybe you see what I'm getting at here. Nimoy's singing was bad. Very, very bad. Seriously bad. Horribly, horribly bad.

The man had made the classic mistake. He had a voice like a bullfrog's, and still thought he could sing. This is something that millions of Americans do every day, with total disregard for the feelings of those around them and for their own personal safety.

If you can't sing, don't sing. It's as simple as that.

Now, maybe you're thinking: Well, how do I *know* if I can't sing? How do I know whether my voice sounds like a mellifluous chorus of angels, or the obnoxious grinding of gears on a city transit bus as it negotiates a particularly steep hill?

The key is audience reaction.

If you're singing a lullaby to your child at bedtime, does he or she suddenly sit bolt upright in bed and begin twitching spasmodically?

While you're riding on the interstate and singing along with the car radio, do your passengers become visibly agitated and ram their heads against the windows and beg to be dropped off at the next exit ramp?

During a rousing chorus of "Happy Birthday," has anyone ever clamped a hand over your mouth and quietly escorted you outside, gently explaining later that "it was for the good of all concerned"?

If so, the odds are excellent that your singing voice is not quite up to snuff, and can be likened to the mournful wailing of a coyote during the mating season, although perhaps a bit more shrill.

Call me a killjoy, but I wouldn't do much singing if your voice inspires this sort of reaction.

Look at what happened to Leonard Nimoy. One minute he's working that Vulcan mind probe on the bridge of the Starship Enterprise, the next minute his career is sinking into obscurity. He could be working a nightclub on the planet Romulus for all you hear of him these days.

I rest my case.

That Barney is such a reptile

Barney the dinosaur's diary:

April 18 — I'm grabbing a smoke outside the studio when that little pain-in-the-neck Tina walks by. Right away she starts gagging and coughing.

"BAR-NEY!" she says in that whiny, irritating voice. "Cigarettes are bad for you!"

"So are the two cheeseburgers you just fired down, tubby," I said. "Now beat it, will ya?"

I'm telling you, sometimes it's all I can do not to backhand these little creeps. Once my contract's up, Jack, I'm outta here. You can take *that* to the bank.

April 20 — Anxiety levels high today. The Barneroo did a mall appearance outside Atlanta. Picture 60,000 little brats jacked up on Cokes and M&M's screaming "BAR-NEY! BAR-NEY!" All these dorky parents pushing camcorders in my face, security guys stepping on my feet, teenage thugs pulling my tail... I thought I was gonna lose it right there.

Three hours without a smoke, too, and they wonder why I snap occasionally and bite off some kid's arm.

April 21 — Took a meeting with the Hasbro toy people. They're interested in developing a new line of Barney products: posters, dolls, action figures, that sort of thing.

Ravitch, my mouthpiece, was laying some preliminary figures on the Hasbro execs when I elbowed him out of the way and said: "Lemme handle this."

"Boys," I said, "let's make this short and sweet. We want a five-year deal, $15 million to sign and 20 percent of the gross profits."

Hasbro's chief negotiator, a big blubbery guy named Riddle, starts sputtering: "B-but that's impossible!"

"Take it or leave it, fatso," I said.

They huddled for a few minutes and then caved in like a mine shaft. I don't know *why* I keep Ravitch on a retainer. All he's ever done for me is post bail a few times.

May 1 — Tell me if this makes sense to you. Universal makes a big-budget movie: "Jurassic Park." It's heavy-duty action-adventure. About clone dinosaurs terrorizing a theme park.

And they don't drop a dime on the Barn-Man? These dopey studio execs don't call the most famous dinosaur on the planet?

Mr. Instant Box Office Bonanza?

Am I missing something here? Hey, it's *their* loss. Just don't come running to me when this thing flops big-time and they're running Steven Spielberg out of town on a rail.

May 10 — I heard Letterman dogged me on his show last night. The guy's really losin' it — I think this move to CBS has him rattled. Anyway, he did some stupid bit: the Top 10 Horrifying Secrets of Barney the Dinosaur. One of them was: Offered Fred Flintstone $1 million for one night with Dino.

Ex-CUSE me? DINO? I don't *think* so. Sharon Stone, maybe. Or that Guess jeans babe, the blonde with the big chest. And don't think I couldn't have my way with either of them. You know what they say: Once you've had a Tyrannosaurus, baby, you never go back.

May 14 — Almost got into it with a couple of those geeks from "Sesame Street." We're doing some promos for PBS when Ernie started ragging me about my voice.

"Sorry," I said, "didn't recognize you without your *boyfriend*. How's old Bert doing, anyway?"

A security guy had to separate us at that point. Ernie's just sore because we're killing him in the ratings.

Then that moron Grover started giving me a hard time until I shouted: "Hey, fur-face, I didn't see *you* at the Clinton inauguration."

May 16 — Oooh, Barney's not feeling so hot today, kids. Might have had a few too many cocktails last night. We had a cast party after the final taping. The kids were chowing down on cake and Hi-C punch and I thought: That's not gonna do it for ol' Barney. So I gave 20 bucks to Jim, one of the stage hands, and he bought me a bottle of Stoli.

Last thing I remember is Sean and Michael carrying me to my dressing room and Lucy telling me to sleep it off. Who's got the aspirin?

May 20 — More bad news: The PBS honchos want me to shill for them during the next pledge-drive beg-a-thon. Yeah, that's all I need: "Hey, boys and girls, go pester mom and dad, OK? Tell 'em to send a hundred bucks pronto or Barney might be going bye-bye."

No wonder these parents hate my guts. You watch. Some lunatic mom is gonna slam a full clip into an M-16 and come looking for me.

Probably at one of these mall gigs.

Come to think of it, there's gotta be a better way to make a living.

Surgeons good enough for celebrities

A friend who had eye surgery not long ago remembers being told that her ophthalmologist was "the same guy who worked on Sugar Ray Leonard's eye."

This is how we measure our surgeons today: What famous patients have they cut open?

We want to hear that our surgeon is the same guy who worked on Orel Hersheiser's arm. Or the same guy who worked on Cher's breasts. Or the same guy who did Larry King's triple bypass. Or — if we're *really* lucky — the same guy who transformed Salman Rushdie from a bearded novelist-in-hiding into a 55-year-old, rosy-cheeked housewife in Surrey.

Understand, I'm not saying Salman Rushdie is, in fact, now living as a 55-year-old rosy-cheeked housewife in Surrey. Although it would make sense to me. What does the man have to lose? At least he'd get out to a restaurant or a movie every once in a while. At least he'd have a decent conversation with someone who wasn't wearing a Scotland Yard ID tag.

The point is, it's only human nature to feel more comfortable with a surgeon whose hands have been entrusted with the bone, tissue, and organs of rich and powerful celebrities.

Whereas, if they're wheeling you into the operating room and you hear someone say of your surgeon "This is the guy who removed the varicose veins from the legs of Marvin Weinstein, that postal carrier down the block," it might not fill you with the same warm feeling of confidence.

Which isn't to say that Marvin Weinstein doesn't deserve the same degree of skill and knowledge from his surgeon as does, say, Marvin Hamlisch.

Marvin Weinstein is a human being. He has thoughts and feelings, does he not?

Marvin Weinstein does not want be lying there on the operating table, only to see his surgeon squash out a Salem and reach for a hip flask just before the anesthesia knocks him out.

And Marvin Weinstein does not want to wake up in post-op with bourbon stains on the sheets and bayonet scars running up and down his legs any more than the next person does.

Salman Rushdie wouldn't stand for that sort of shoddy surgery (if he were ever to have surgery, transsexual or otherwise. Remember, I didn't state categorically that he did).

Why should Marvin Weinstein be any different?

Getting back to my friend who had the eye surgery, she felt much better knowing her doctor was considered so good that he had been retained by a famous prize fighter (and former soft drink spokesman, we should mention that).

Still, it begs the question: What did they tell Sugar Ray Leonard when *he* first started shopping around for an ophthalmologist?

Obviously, there was no doctor then known as "the same guy who worked on Sugar Ray Leonard's eye." What if the doctor recommended to Sugar Ray hadn't operated on any famous patients at all?

Imagine if the sole reassurance they could give Sugar Ray was: "Well, your surgeon is the guy who worked on Constance W. Barbieri's detached retina. Constance works in the Junior Miss department at Sears."

Maybe you see what I'm getting at here.

If I'm Sugar Ray, I want to see something a little more impressive on my doctor's resume than: "Repaired Connie Barbieri's retina. Patient returned to work at Sears; transferred to light fixtures dept. when eyesight improved dramatically."

On the other hand, if I heard that my ophthalmologist is the same guy who saved Oprah Winfrey's eyesight after a grueling seven-hour cornea transplant, I would feel a whole hell of a lot better.

Understand, I'm not saying Oprah did, in fact, undergo major eye surgery. Then again, I'm not saying she didn't. (What's she hiding, anyway? Why doesn't she just schedule a news conference and clear up this whole thing before the tabloids get a hold of it? I can see the headlines now: GREEDY TALK SHOW HOST TO DYING ORPHAN: "GIVE ME YOUR EYES, DAMMIT!")

Are you kidding? The tabloids would pounce on that story like a dog shaking a bone. An army of network TV people would be camped on her front lawn. Lifestyle reporters from every major newspaper would be calling her at all hours of the day and night.

The woman's hair would be falling out by the third day of the siege.

No. I wouldn't want that on my conscience.

Bad days in Little Rock

Al Gore's diary:

Nov. 4, 1992 — Ohhhhh... my head is pounding. Got a major-league hangover. The victory party last night was completely out of control. Clinton was mixing pitcher after pitcher of kamikazes. I was happy sipping an Amstel Light and talking about chlorofluorocarbons and the ozone layer with Ron Brown. Then Bill stumbled over and got me in a headlock and shrieked: "When Bill Clinton drinks, *everybody* drinks!"

The next thing I know, Herve Villechez is sitting on my lap and everyone's throwing confetti and screaming: "Ze plane! Ze plane!"

God, it was awful! Tipper says she hasn't seen anything like that since keg party days at college.

Nov. 5 — Someone kicked in the bedroom door at 5:30 this morning and in barged Clinton and five Secret Service agents, all dressed in sweatsuits. Tipper pulled the blankets around her and started screaming like they had just escaped from San Quentin.

"Get up!" Bill barked. "We're going jogging."

I said: "Bill, for God's sake, the sun isn't even..."

"I don't like this any better than you do," he said, peering out the window. "But we gotta make it look good for the photographers."

So we went out jogging in the rain and I nearly got hit by a bus. Is this what the next four years are gonna be like? Because if they are, I want out right now.

Nov. 8 — Practiced standing very still in front of a mirror and staring admiringly at a picture of Bill taped to the wall.

I thought I stood real still at his first post-election news conference. But Bill said the videotapes showed me brushing my hair from my forehead at one point. Apparently, I also took my eyes off him once or twice to look out at the press.

Tipper says to look on the bright side, that I can always get a job as a department store mannequin when I'm out of politics.

Nov. 10 — Dan Quayle called this morning. He was bawling like a baby. Said he can't bear the thought of stepping down as VP, that he'll probably wind up working in a Rite-Aid, stocking the shelves with Mylanta.

He said being VP is the easiest gig in the world. All you do every day is put on a dark suit and check the obits to see what world leader died. Then you jump on a plane, say a few prayers in front of the stiff's coffin, and it's back to the Cairo Hilton or wherever for cocktails and dinner.

Quayle said if they ever advertised the VP's job in the Help Wanted ads, there'd be so many applicants you'd have to beat them off with fire hoses and attack dogs.

Nov. 13 — This is getting ridiculous. Bill barged in at 5:15 this morning and had the Secret Service guys pull me out of bed. Tipper started screaming again and Bill told her to shut her yap, that we were just going jogging.

For the record, I was against this whole idea of living at the governor's mansion in the first place, transition period or no transition period.

Nov. 16 — Finally got up the nerve to ask Bill what he uses on his hair. I mean, it *never* moves! Turns out it's a secret substance that's one part Wildroot to three parts Rustoleum. But he said he's thinking of switching to an industrial-strength shellac used for gymnasium floors.

Nov. 20 — I... I don't know how much more of this I can take. Someone's shaking me at 4:30 in the morning and I look up and it's Bill. "C'mon," he said, "we gotta go for a jog. Ted Koppel and his camera crew are outside."

Thank God Tipper didn't wake up. Or maybe she did, but at least she didn't scream. Bill was right — the duct tape over her mouth works real well.

Nov. 24 — Bill caught me jabbing Socks the cat with the fireplace poker again. He said he was "disappointed" in me.

I told him I've been under a lot of stress lately. Mainly from lack of sleep — *someone* keeps bursting into my bedroom at dawn and dragging me out to go jogging.

Nov. 26 — We all sat down to Thanksgiving dinner together, although God knows what I have to be thankful for in this nut house. Chelsea caused a big scene, whining about how she wouldn't eat any dark meat and then kicking the maid.

I'm telling you, this kid is gonna make Amy Carter look like Shirley Temple. I hope Bill and Hillary aren't surprised when her head starts spinning 360 degrees and she floats up to the ceiling.

Nov. 27 — That's it — I gotta get out of Little Rock. What a hick town. I swear the cars here still have running boards on them. Some folks told me "The Jack Paar Show" is still the top-rated TV program here.

Although, they added, it's getting pushed hard by "The Mod Squad."

Gimme Money — That's What I Want

A lazy man's career track

Our support group for the chronically lazy meets every other Thursday at St. Theresa's Elementary School, provided Ty Harrington gets off his duff and gets us a key to the side door.

I missed our last meeting — just didn't feel like getting off the couch — but they tell me it went pretty much like all the rest as far as the bickering is concerned.

Sarah Mullins was supposed to bring the coffee and doughnuts, but then decided it was too much trouble, so there were no refreshments to speak of.

Then there was a problem with the seating. Usually we sit on folding chairs, but everyone figured it was a hassle to pull the chairs out of the janitor's closet — especially if they were going to make us put them back after the meeting.

So the group ended up leaning against the stage for two hours, which apparently was pretty darn uncomfortable. At one point, Carmine Melello stood and said "This is ridiculous!" and went off to get some chairs.

But he never came back and, sure enough, at the end of the meeting they found him asleep on a couch in the principal's office. Carmine, he just might be the laziest person in the group, at least I assume he is, not having bothered to check.

All I heard when I was growing up was how lazy I was and how I'd never amount to anything.

In fact, the enduring memory of my teen-age years is my mother barging into my bedroom every morning and yelling: "WHEN ARE YOU GETTING A JOB?!"

"HEY, HAVE A LITTLE CONSIDERATION!" I'd yell back. "IT'S 11 O'CLOCK. PEOPLE ARE TRYING TO SLEEP!"

Let's face it, the last thing you want to do is get in a shouting match with your mom, especially when you need her to drop you off at the pool hall later. But sometimes Mom was out of control. And just because she only needed eight hours of sleep, it didn't mean the rest of the world had the same biological makeup.

Perhaps the defining moment in my lifelong problem with laziness occurred at the age of 17 while applying for a job as a lifeguard.

At first glance, the job looked to be right up my alley. I figured all you did was sit in a big white chair on the beach with a whistle around your neck and a dab of zinc oxide on your nose while leering at the girls in their bikinis.

If a swimmer were actually in trouble, it seemed to me you could always turn to your partner and say something like: "Teddy, get that guy for me, will ya? Yeah, the one in the red trunks. Just went under."

But during my job interview, the supervisor of lifeguards ruined everything by announcing: "We're looking for people who aren't afraid of hard work."

And I thought: "Oh, God, not another one of these fanatics like Mom."

Well, it turned out this guy was a real head case. Not only were the lifeguards expected to jump in the surf themselves to save floundering swimmers, they were also expected to police the beach and pick up any stray bottles and cans. Plus you were expected to be on the job six hours a day.

To make a long story short, I didn't get the job. The lifeguard supervisor said he didn't like my "attitude," whatever that meant. (Someone told me later he got annoyed when I put my head down on his desk and took a nap, although my asking for two weeks vacation "up front" might have put him off, too, I suppose.)

From there, I drifted from one failed job opportunity to another, marking a steady downward descent until I ultimately landed with a thud in a humor writer's position.

For a chronically lazy person, the job is a godsend, allowing one to engage in sophomoric discourses on the most juvenile of topics, holier-than-thou posturing and all manner of wild and irresponsible accusations — all done (and this is the part I really like) with little or no research.

Getting back to the support group, however, it has certainly become a meaningful influence in my life.

At our next meeting, we're scheduled to discuss plans for a raffle and dinner dance in the spring. This would involve group members going door-to-door and selling a minimum of six books of raffle tickets each, as well as devoting time and energy toward renting a banquet hall, planning a menu, hiring a band, etc.

Me, I wouldn't book a baby-sitter just yet.

A healthy way to call in sick

Today we tackle the delicate subject of how to call in sick at work, providing you really *are* sick, which of course, you are. I don't mean to imply any dishonesty on your part.

First of all, pay no attention to fellow employees who claim to have never been sick a day in their lives.

Because you know what happens to people like that? They get hit by a bus.

Or a piano drops 15 stories onto their head.

And then at the funeral everyone stands around and says: "Poor old Harry. He was never sick a day in his life."

It never fails. The minute you hear someone was never sick a day in his life, you can pretty much assume he checked out in some bizarre way, such as his cat ate him or something.

It reminds me of all those interviews they do after a mass murderer has been arrested.

The guy's landlord always says: "Well, he was a loner. He kept pretty much to himself."

It's gotten so that the minute I hear the word "loner," I picture a guy in a camouflage jacket walking into a grocery store with an M-16.

Just once I'd like to hear the mass murderer's landlord say: "He was a gregarious sort, the life of the party. He was always singing and dancing, and did this great impression of Sammy Davis, Jr."

But no, the guy's always hanging out by himself in a basement apartment.

Probably never sick a day in his life, either.

But getting back to our subject, which was actually not mass murderers but rather how to call in sick, this is how the average Joe does it.

He gets the boss on the phone. And in a weak voice he says: "Hello, Mr. Grimes? This is (cough) Evans. I don't think I can (cough, cough) come in today. I (cough) must have caught a bug."

All of which is probably causing Grimes to think: Boy, is that lame.

Because Grimes wasn't born yesterday. He's going to see right through that act, incorrectly assuming you have just thrown your golf clubs in the trunk and are now peeling out of the driveway.

I'm not saying you have to be DeNiro on the phone, but for God's sake put a little effort into it.

For instance, throw a couple of sniffles in there. And sneezes. Bosses love to hear sneezes. A good sneeze, especially one of uncommon pitch and violence, lends a certain legitimacy to complaints of ill health.

You may even wish to have your wife call in sick for you. This implies you're so ill you can't even get out of bed and have to have your wife alibi (although that's not the word) for you.

One note of caution: Make sure your symptoms match the illness you're describing, although I'm sure they do. After all, you're sick, you're not making this up.

For instance, it would not do to inform the boss you have a sore throat and have likely contracted cholera.

Number one, cholera is a bacterial disease that strikes the intestines and is characterized by severe diarrhea.

Number two, it has been virtually wiped out in this country, although it is still endemic in parts of the Far East. So this story would sound genuine only in the event you were, say, a shipping clerk in Hong Kong.

I myself would stick to less exotic illnesses, although you certainly know your boss better than I do. Lord knows he's been on your back long enough.

A lot of people assume that once they call in sick, that's the end of the matter.

Nothing could be farther from the truth. Because when you come back to work, you must retain some vestiges of the illness, which, again, was legitimate and certainly nothing you should be ashamed of.

But it wouldn't do to come strolling into the office the morning after your absence looking tanned and fit, as if you just played 18 holes of golf — which of course you didn't — and casually announce that your agonizing bout with gastroenteritis was "a twelve-hour thing."

Grimes can't be that stupid.

No one can be that stupid.

Because people with gastroenteritis tend not to acquire a healthy tan, as they are generally doubled over in pain in some hospital bed, howling for morphine or for someone to just shoot them in the temple and get it over with.

So at least remember to clutch your stomach as you slip away to the water cooler to tell the one about the bartender and the monkey.

And keep telling everybody: A less dedicated employee would still be in the hospital.

Job prospects then and now

Today's column is directed at you recent college graduates, who will now take your hard-earned degrees in teaching and accounting and chemical engineering and put them to good use pushing burritos at Taco Bell.

Yeah, I saw those cheery headlines the other day: "CLASS OF '93 FACES CRUEL JOB MARKET! WORST EMPLOYMENT SCENE IN 20 YEARS AWAITS COLLEGE GRADS!"

Boy, that'll really make you want to jump out of bed in the morning, huh? No wonder you people are out every night until 2 a.m. at keg parties and wet T-shirt contests and satanic rituals in the middle of deserted cemeteries. Why turn in early if the only thing you have to look forward to is another day sprawled on a lumpy couch watching "McGyver" re-runs?

What you graduates have to realize is that they say the same thing every year about the job market.

Every year is supposed to be the worst one in history for graduating college seniors seeking jobs. Just once I'd like to pick up a newspaper in May and read: "JOBS PLENTIFUL FOR NEW GRADS, MEDIAN STARTING SALARY $80,000. MOST COMPANIES THROWING IN FREE CARS."

If it makes you graduates feel any better, the job market is just as shaky today as when I got out of journalism school in the mid-'70s.

As this was shortly after the Watergate scandals, journalism schools were bursting with bright-eyed, aggressive Woodward and Bernstein clones, eager to bring about the downfall of the president of the United States — or, barring that, to hound and badger public officials, engage in reckless witch hunts of authority figures, and irritate the general public.

Well, it sure sounded like fun to me.

But strangely enough, newspapers at that time weren't clamoring to hire a long-haired guy with zero ambition who didn't want to get out of bed before ten in the morning because he was out till all hours of the night playing softball and drinking beer with his buddies.

Me, I couldn't get over the *attitude* of these newspapers.

Here I was, willing to bust my tail for four or five hours a day — except, of course, weekends and holidays, which is when we had our softball tournaments — and *still* they kept sending my resumes back with the smarmy notation: "We are looking for someone a bit more committed."

Well, thank you very much! You don't think that hurt my feelings? For weeks I moped around the house with weepy eyes, barely able to make it to my lumpy couch each morning for another round of "The Price Is Right."

But I showed them. I took all the writing and reporting skills I had accumulated at school and promptly found a job as ... a bartender.

As you can imagine, this sort of a career move really thrilled my mother.

Every once in a while, Mom would come in the bar and look at me and think: "Yeah, there's my son. Look what four years of college did for him. Look at how well he pours that draft beer into that mug! And the snappy way he cleans out those ash trays! And look ... look how he pushed that drunk's head out of the way so he could wipe down the bar! No question about it: I couldn't be prouder of the boy!"

Eventually, though, I landed a job as a reporter at a medium-sized daily newspaper, which any sensible person would recognize as a step down from bartending.

People were coming up and congratulating me on my new job, which I didn't understand at all. Not only was I having less fun, making less money and meeting fewer women, but now I had to deal with all those pain-in-the-neck editors.

At one point I thought: "Gee, if I get any more successful, I might need anti-depressants."

But maybe times are even tougher now for graduating seniors, if that's possible. The other day I read in the newspaper about an economics major from a large college in Maryland.

Since he hasn't yet lined up a job, he planned to begin his post-academic career mowing lawns.

Mowing lawns! Isn't that the kind of job you look for in eighth grade?!

What's next for this poor guy, a sidewalk lemonade stand? Setting up a rickety bridge table with a crude cardboard sign, a half-dozen Dixie cups, and a pitcher of watery Country Time mix?

Harassing neighbors and passers-by with annoying cries of: "Hey, get yer lemonade here! Ice cold lemonade!"? Living (if that's the word) on the proceeds of a business that takes in a nickel a cup and three cents for refills?

I don't know ... it seems like an awful lot of stress to me.

Some jobs take a huge toll

Having just returned from an extensive car trip through five states, I'm considering a career move that some may find startling, but which makes perfect sense to a man bent on reducing the stress in his life: toll collector.

From what I've been able to observe, basically the job description reads this way:

1. Stick hand out toll booth.
2. Take money from motorist.
3. Put money in till/make change.
4. Repeat Step 1.

Eight pressure-free hours later, boom, you're waving goodbye to your co-workers and gunning the Camaro toward the nearest tavern.

And I'm guessing you don't bring the job home with you, either. That evening around the dinner table, there's no talk about how you screwed up the O'Mara account or how the bond market took a nose dive.

Even if something *did* go wrong down at the toll plaza — say you misplaced a roll of quarters — you probably won't beat yourself over the head all night because of it.

Oh, sure, occasionally a motorist might throw your rhythm off by asking for directions to a local landmark such as Walt's Famous World of Reptiles.

But all you do there is roll your eyes to the heavens and mutter (in your most world-weary and disinterested voice): "Three exits up, follow the signs to Route 40."

Then, unless the traffic's backed up to Key West, you go back to your Sidney Sheldon novel or your dog-eared copy of *Field and Stream*. Or finish watching a "M*A*S*H" re-run on your four-inch portable TV.

I could do that. In fact, there's every...

OK, I know what's going to happen here. The mail's going to bring all sorts of letters from irate toll collectors, who, working some lonely toll plaza on I-95 at 3 A.M., will turn the volume down on their Sony Walkmans long enough to scribble: "THIS IS A DAMN TOUGH JOB, MISTER!" on Highway Department stationery. With the word "tough" underlined three times for emphasis.

To which I would respond: EX-CUSE ME? You think *you* have it tough? Try going through life as a humor writer, which in the newspaper business is sort of like eating off a tv tray while the adults in the next room sit down to dinner at a banquet table.

There are times (more than you'll ever know) when I must bang my head furiously against a filing cabinet for several minutes in order to get the creative juices flowing.

You do that three or four times a week, 47 or so weeks per year, and your head gradually assumes the mushy, irregular shape of an over-ripe cantaloupe.

The pounding takes its toll in so many other ways besides ill-defined skull texture, too.

Slurred speech, disorientation, six-inch gashes along the scalp line, uncontrolled drooling, flecks of dried blood mixed with gunmetal-gray filing cabinet paint in the hair — all have visited me at one time or another after a particularly trying session of summoning the muse.

So don't tell me about job hazards, Mr. or Ms. Toll Collector. I don't want to hear it, OK? Your, ahem, *job* is a piece of cake compared to the hell I go through turning out three dreary columns per week.

(BAM! BAM! There, I just slammed my head into a wall here at the office. Not a pretty sight, believe me. Uh-oh, must have startled the woman at the next desk. Three people are rushing over with handkerchiefs now to stanch the bleeding.)

(BAM! But this is the price you pay if you want to write humor. BAM! Do you toll collectors have to do this? Huh? When someone hands you a buck and you owe them 60 cents change, do you freeze in front of the till and finally throw up your hands and cry: "I... I CAN'T DO THIS!"?)

I think not. Happens to me all the time, though. Horrible, agonizing bouts of writer's block, where my self-confidence plummets like a steel-bucket down a deep well and...

But enough about me. What's the worst way a toll collector can screw up on the job?

You give a motorist too much change? Or it turns out Walt's Famous World of Reptiles is *four* exits up the interstate, not three, and on Route 50, *not* Route 40?

Big deal. Your boss isn't going to know there's money missing unless he sees you walking to your car with a laundry sack stuffed with tens and twenties.

And as for those folks trying frantically to find Walt's Famous World of Reptiles, well, Walt's a broken-down has-been in the reptile-farm game. The whole business where he climbs in a cage with 20 pit vipers is done with mirrors.

Or so I hear.

Don't be silly, quit and retire

"We're going to buy a house, a boat, a Harley Davidson motorcycle and two new cars." — Mark Gaydos, who, along with his wife Sherry, recently won $4.8 million in Maryland's Lotto game.

The article about the newest lottery winners appeared in a roundup section of the local rag, and I read it expecting the usual claptrap about putting the money in the bank or saving it for the kids' college education, blah, blah, blah.

This is the sort of nonsense that traditionally emanates from the mouths of lottery winners.

The TV lights click on and a lottery official hands them the ceremonial four-foot check and the winners get this vacant, Stepford Wives look in their eyes as they intone: "How'll we spend it? Well, Emma and I will probably fix up the chicken coop in the back and put the rest of the money in some sort of retirement account."

Then I came across the wonderful quote above from Mark Gaydos and I thought: Finally! Here is the person I've been looking for. Here is a man who knows what to do with 4.8 million bucks, who will indulge himself, who will have some *fun*.

I'm telling you, it nearly brought tears to my eyes.

Gaydos' quote was especially refreshing because the first thing so many of these lottery winners say after hitting the big payoff is: "Well, the money won't change *me*."

This is an absolutely incredible statement, yet it's made all the time, with the same wide-eyed innocence normally found only in those under the age of seven.

All I can say is, you would notice a lot of changes in me if *I* won nearly 5 million bucks!

The first change you'd notice would be me laughing hysterically and guzzling champagne (which I don't even like) and swinging from the nearest chandelier for several days.

Soon, you would notice other changes, such as the new Mercedes in the driveway and the "For Sale" sign in front of my house.

Another thing all these big-time lottery winners say is that they're going to keep their jobs.

I can't tell you how many times I've heard some guy who's just won $10 million say: "Oh, yeah, I'll be back at Mr. Tire first thing in the morning. I love my job. And I'd miss my friends if I quit."

When I hear this kind of talk, it takes all the willpower I have not to jump in the car, drive over to that person's house, and bash a two-by-four over his head in the hope of bringing him to his senses.

Then I want to grab him by the lapels and say: "Listen, pal, if you're so hung up on tires, take some of that $10 million and buy yourself a Firestone dealership. That way you can be around tires all you want without having to pick up an air gun every day and break your back on the lug nuts of a '76 Mustang.

"Plus you won't be spending your days wondering: Is it the left rear rim that gets the new tire and the right front that gets the spare? Or vice-versa?

"As for missing your friends, look, with that kind of money, you can *buy* new friends. That's the whole point of friendship. Hell, *I'll* be your friend right now."

Let me tell you something. If I ever won 10 million bucks, my editors would see me sprinting out of the office with four pieces of Samsonite luggage and plane tickets to Martinique in my back pocket.

And that would be the last they'd ever see of me. Maybe I'd send a postcard, but I doubt it.

Happily, both Mark and Sherry Gaydos are displaying uncommon good sense retiring from their jobs, which collectively earned them around $45,000 a year.

It was also heartening to see that the Gaydoses will spend their money on cars, boats, motorcycles and the like, since so many of these big lottery winners insist on spending the money so sensibly.

Over and over, we hear these people chanting the same tired mantra: "Well, we're putting the money away for the kids' college education."

Tell me something: What the hell kind of attitude is *that?!* Lighten up! Buy a mansion or take a trip around the world. Or throw a big party — and not the kind where people have to pass around the Cheez Whiz and pump the keg next to the ping-pong table.

Listen, you think the kids are worrying about you? You think they're over at the mall right now puffing Marlboros and shuffling though the video arcade with the rest of their green-haired friends and thinking: "Gee, I wonder if Mom and Dad have enough money to retire?"

That'll be the day.

Food for thought — but no change

The day began unraveling when I put 60 cents in the vending machine at work, pressed the button for Diet Coke and nothing happened.

As a writer of sorts, I recognized that there was much symbolism here. The emptiness of life, the wretchedness of the human condition — it was all staring me in the face.

So I hit the buttons for Coke, Sprite, Sunkist Orange, and iced tea, and nothing happened. Then I hit the coin return lever and nothing happened. The nothingness was overwhelming. And I knew: the nothingness was a metaphor for *something*.

I now moved on to the candy machine because I am not a quitter, and because the symbolism was coming hot and heavy. I put in 55 cents and pushed the button for Peanut M&M's and nothing happened.

When I pushed the buttons for a Mr. Goodbar, Snickers or Reese's peanut butter cups, nothing happened then either.

Then I noticed a large white piece of paper taped to the side of the machine, on which was scrawled: "Out of Order."

The paper symbolized hope, anyone could see that. The shaky cursive writing represented the defiling of all that is pure.

I wasn't sure what the tape represented. Ambiguity, perhaps. Although that's just off the top of my head.

As to the words "Out of Order"... yes, heavy symbolism there. Isn't the whole *system* out of order?

Once upon a time, you could count on certain things: a hearty, cholesterol-laden breakfast, the Yankees in first place, a thriving war-based economy, the love of a good woman (or man, if you leaned toward that sex).

Now what do we have? Chaos, Bran flakes, a team from Canada winning the World Series, no nukes and no jobs, and people who whine about how romance will affect their *careers*.

People have become so *annoying*, haven't they? Little things, like the bank teller in the mousy brown cardigan who chirps "All righty!" when you say you'd like to cash a check.

ALL RIGHTY?! What kind of talk is that?

And what about the person who ends every sentence with the word "'kay?" I know a woman, Fran F. (not her real initial), who does that: "We were at the movies, 'kay? And Gary went to get some popcorn, 'kay? So I'm just sitting there, 'kay? And this man comes in and..."

I'll tell you this: I am not a violent man. But if you listen to Fran for more than a minute or two, the lyrics to "Helter Skelter" start screaming in your head and you find yourself edging toward the silverware drawer.

So now I moved on to the coffee machine, my spirits deflating like a tire with a slow leak, if you can appreciate the imagery there.

The coffee machine is one of those sleek, ultramodern deals that looks like the instrument panel on the Nautilus submarine. It allows you to order coffee in any imaginable configuration: with cream, with sugar, with cream and sugar, with LoCal substitute, decaf, etc.

This surfeit of choices represented... what? Futility? The institutionalized blandness predicted in Orwell's *1984?* I don't know. To be honest, I was getting tired of all the symbolism.

I put my 35 cents in and punched the buttons for cream and LoCal substitute. This time the machine whirred into action. A steaming cup of java appeared behind the little plastic door.

It tasted... awful. Oh, the cream was there, but no LoCal substitute. As I am addicted to the sickeningly sweet taste of saccharin, the stuff that makes laboratory rats keel over on their little treadmills, I threw the cup in the trash.

The trash represented... I don't know. The plight of the dispossessed? The linkage between the Joad family in Steinbeck's *The Grapes of Wrath* and today's... well, never mind. I'm sorry I brought the whole thing up.

There was nothing left to do except begin the long, lonely walk back to my desk. The desk at least represented stability. If anybody even *cares* at this point.

Back upstairs, someone offered me a stick of chewing gum.

I said: "Is this the stick that sat on the dashboard of your car for two months, baking in the hot sun and oozing into the defroster vent until one day you casually threw it in the change carrier near the stick shift, where it gathered hair, fuzz, cigarette ashes and God knows what else before your husband finally cleaned the car and tossed it in the glove compartment with the ice scraper, travel packet of Kleenex and map of Pennsylvania? And now you expect *me* to put it in my mouth?!"

"I... I bought the gum this morning," she stammered.

So I took it and chewed it. It was just... OK.

Like so much of life these days, I suppose.

A Bronx cheer for the cheerful

Tell me, is there anything more irritating than people who are relentlessly cheerful in the morning?

I'm talking about those people who begin each day with a broad smile and a gooey Richard Simmons-like perkiness no matter how ungodly the hour.

I'm talking about those people who exhibit boundless energy and unfailing good humor without having to down 27 cups of strong coffee.

God, I hate those people.

I hate the holier-than-thou tone behind their good spirits. I hate the way they flaunt their cheerfulness at a time when others can barely put one foot in front of the other.

Remember chirpy Florence Henderson in that Wesson oil commercial a few years ago?

Remember her raking her pinky through the Wesson, licking it and flashing a big, goofy smile at the camera, like it was the greatest thing she'd ever tasted? And remember her gushing on and on about "Wesson-ality," to the point where you wanted to shake her and scream: "Florence! For God's sake, it's *cooking oil!*"

That's the kind of insufferable cheerfulness we're talking about here — a cheerfulness entirely inappropriate for the occasion.

Frankly, it has always been my position that cheerfulness in and of itself should not be permitted before a certain hour (say, eleven a.m.), and then only in measured doses.

Anything more will grate on the nerves of those around the cheerful person, and people will begin to regard him or her as a kook or a closet amphetamine freak.

Some years ago, I worked with a reporter who would bound into the office early each morning with a look of pure joy on her face.

As soon as she reached her desk, she would sing out: "Isn't it a great, great day?!"

This is what the woman said, without fail, every day.

Every single day.

Every single day for six long months.

Think about that for a moment.

I don't know if I can describe how annoying this phrase became, except to say that a number of reporters would begin howling and bashing their heads against the filing cabinets as soon as they heard it.

Putting aside for the moment the bizarre neo-Pavlovian response of her colleagues, the woman was just too damn cheerful for her own good.

It was like sitting across from Mary Poppins, minus the bumbershoot. After a while, you wanted to strangle her.

One morning, as she was bustling about the office in her usual Little Miss Sunshine mode, I took her aside.

"Tell me," I said, lowering my voice to a whisper, "what kind of drugs are you on? C'mon, you can trust me."

For a moment, she seemed genuinely puzzled.

"What is it? Dexedrine?" I inquired. "Two hundred milligrams? Is that why you bounce around here like a Labrador retriever who's been cooped up for days?"

"I... I don't take any..."

"Or is it one of the Beta-blockers, like Inderol?" I continued. "Or a tricyclic anti-depressant that..."

"Look," she said sharply, "it's not drugs. I meditate every morning."

"Let me see if I've got this straight," I said. "You buzz around here every morning like Maria Von Trapp on three bottles of Vivarin — and all that comes from meditation?"

"Yes," she said. "Meditation has enriched my life tremendously."

The woman actually talked like that. That was another reason people had vivid dreams of creeping up behind her with a length of garroting wire.

Anyway, the bottom line on this meditating business was that she spent 45 minutes each morning practicing an offshoot of TM — transcendental meditation.

This, she said, allowed her "inner reservoir" to overflow with tremendous energy each morning. (Personally, I felt she could have banged back four or five cups of Folgers and saved herself a lot of time.)

Nevertheless, when informed that her perkiness had become extremely annoying, she promised not to be so overtly cheerful, and she proved true to her word. In fact, pretty soon she was as sour and grumpy as the rest of us in the morning. Morale in the newsroom improved markedly.

Now, what exactly am I trying to say here?

Am I saying there is *never* a need for the kind of zany, rake-a-pinky-through-the Wesson bubbliness pioneered by Florence Henderson?

Yes, that's *exactly* what I'm saying.

Oh, the shopping you could do

This came to me in the mall one day as we walked past Just Shower Caps and Hal's House of Plaids and the bench where the disaffected young people with green hair and nose rings hang out smoking Salems.

A refrigerator magnet store. No, hear me out. Call it something cutesy like, oh, Stick to Me. Or maybe Fridge Friends.

Twelve hundred feet of floor space is what I'm thinking. Row after row after row of refrigerator magnets gleaming under the track lighting, everything from those little fruit jobs and "I Love My Grandma" messages to the more elaborate magnets with the Ansel Adams scenes etched in polyurethane.

Look at the hassle you go through now to buy a refrigerator magnet.

Maybe you go to one of those gourmet kitchen stores where they make you wade through spatulas and pot holders while an officious woman in a white apron with her hair in a bun shoots you dirty looks if you even *brush* against the oven mitts.

Or you go to a discount store like K-mart, where you're liable to run into someone's senile 82-year-old grandfather rolling a radial tire down the aisle while sniffing a can of wood sealant. Who needs *that*?

The point is, the age of specialization is here, pal. Do one thing and do it well. Especially in malls. Hey, I hear a certain famous chain of beefstick-and-cheese salons (no names, please) is thinking about dropping its whole line of smoked sausage and going just with cheese. Maybe only *Muenster* cheese, too. Can you imagine?

Anyway, the other idea I had is Strictly Terriers, which would be pretty much what the name implies.

At long last you'd have a pet store devoted to one of the hottest breed of dogs around. Nothing in the store but terriers (Airedale, fox, Scotch, Jack Russell, you name it) and terrier-related products: custom-made leashes and collars, how-to books on raising your terrier, I (Heart) My Terrier bumper stickers, gag books like *Terrier Spoken Here.*

There would also be a bulletin board near the cash register crammed with news from the terrier breeder world, as well as addresses and phone numbers of terrier aficionados in your area. Someone comes in looking for a beagle or something, you show him the door.

"You want the Beagle Barn," you say politely but firmly. "Up the escalator and to the left, next to Sears."

Pretty soon, each time the little bell above the door jingles, you'll know it's not someone looking for iguana food or one of those pecking bars for parakeets.

I'll tell you something else that would be huge in a mall: a shrink. There are a lot of miserable people out there and we're not doing enough to get them off the streets and into the malls where they belong. Not to mention where they might spend a few bucks and get our economy moving in the right direction.

Anyway, you go with a '90s theme here and call the shrink's office something like, oh, Mind Games. No, maybe that's too flip. How about What's Yer Problem? No, too... I don't know, *challenging*.

Wait a minute! Phobias N' Things. There you go.

Now, unlike Strictly Terriers, you'd want to expand the focus a little and treat a broad range of problems: anxiety, depression, mood swings, food dysfunctions, simple shyness, etc.

At least for the first few months, advertising would be an imperative. You'd want a lot of signs in the front window geared to mall traffic, such as:

"Unsettling Dreams Interpreted While U Wait!"

"Complete Jungian Analysis in 30 Minutes or Your Money Back!"

"Ask About Our Rebates for Multiple-Personality Disorders!"

Look, the place should be nothing fancy. We'd go with standard-issue waiting room furniture in muted gray tones and year-old *People* magazines. Maybe a nice aquarium off to one side — the emotionally distressed are said to find fish soothing.

The therapist's office would be a similarly no-frills set-up: two lumpy chairs, couch, glass coffee table with the requisite copy of *Architectural Digest,* artificial plant in the corner.

And get this: For those patients who demand privacy, at the end of a session, instead of exiting through the waiting room, they'd go through a breezeway that leads into the Burger King next door!

Is that neat or what? Again, the goal is not necessarily to help these patients, but to get them in the mall where they might patronize the other stores.

Speaking of Burger King, it probably goes without saying that we should jazz up some of these food courts. One possible direction — I'm just thinking out loud here — involves Thai food. Nobody these days is doing Thai.

Check out these women

After years of exhaustive research, I have discovered the basic difference between men and women shoppers.

Men have their money ready to pay the cashier. Women never do.

I hope that doesn't sound like too much of a generalization, but there are facts to back it up — not that I personally have any.

But from what I've observed, your basic woman can hold up a checkout line better than a bomb threat called in from the corner pay phone.

A woman will wait ten minutes in a checkout line with a bottle of Pepsi.

Finally she reaches the cashier.

She waits until the cashier says something like: "That'll be $1.29."

Then — and only then — will a woman reach for her wallet.

It's as if a little light bulb goes off in her head, like you see in the cartoons, and she remembers: "Oh, yes. I have to pay for this. With U.S. currency. I'd better get it now. The cashier seems to be waiting."

It's a most amazing thing to watch, even better than cable TV at two in the morning.

But I will tell you what is even more amazing.

Let's say the woman is not paying for a purchase with cash.

Let's say that, after waiting in a checkout line for ten minutes, she decides — the very thought makes me shudder — to pay with a check.

This is a process which can take longer than photosynthesis.

If I can stay awake long enough to detail it, it goes something like this:

The woman reaches into her pocketbook.

She pulls out a checkbook.

She borrows a pen from the cashier.

She starts to make out the check.

She asks the cashier for the date.

The cashier says, um, let me see, June 28.

The cashier says, um, I need to see your driver's license.

The woman says: Oh, God, where did I put that?

And on and on and on it goes, to the point where the rest of the people in line break out cots and blankets and try to grab some shut-eye until this woman is through.

In fact, when I think of it, it's unfair to compare the process to photosynthesis, as green plants convert sunlight to chemical energy in a matter of hours.

Whereas this business with the checkbook can take all day.

Now, without trying to pat anyone on the back here, let's look at your garden-variety male shopper.

This guy is usually not happy about being in a store in the first place.

He knows he's out of his element. And he knows if he hangs around too long, he's only going to screw up a purchase or run over somebody's kid with a shopping cart.

So when he finally reaches the cashier, it's like having one foot over the barbed wire atop the Berlin Wall.

He can smell freedom and he's ready to flee. So he's got the money in his hand — often the exact change — and an alert expression on his face. He's all business.

So now let's say the cashier says: "That'll be $2.95."

Bingo. The guy drops three bills in her hand, grabs his nickel change and sprints to the parking lot.

The whole exchange takes maybe 30 seconds. And he doesn't have 30 people behind him cursing under their breath and hoping he rams his car into a tree.

Here is another difference between men and women shoppers: Women consider shopping therapeutic. Well, some of them do. At least the one I live with does.

I noticed this the other day when I asked her to please move my weights from the basement to the attic. Notice I used the word "please." It seemed like a nice touch.

But for some reason, this simple request enraged her. She stormed out of the house, returning later with so many packages I thought she had knocked over a Federal Express van.

She said shopping helps "defuse" her anger.

"Oh, yeah?" I said. "How about if I '*defuse*' to pay for all this stuff?"

Therapy or no therapy, you better have a snappy comeback when they're driving you to the poor house.

The same thing happened when I asked her to change a flat on my Toyota.

You would have thought I asked her to move the refrigerator. Which I didn't — at least not by herself. I got her sister to help.

But sure enough, we had a terrific argument. She told me to get lost, which I did. And when I returned home that day, the place was so cluttered with shopping bags it looked like Christmas Eve.

I hope she didn't hold up too many people in the checkout line.

Although I wouldn't bet against it.

Last Call at the 7-Eleven

Supermarkets are where the real action is

It is Friday evening and I am in the supermarket fingering a boneless bottom round roast, tiny shivers of delight rippling up my spine.

According to the sticker, the boneless bottom round sells for two thick lines, one thin line and three thicks.

"That's not bad," I say to a woman nearby. "Anywhere else, this baby goes for three thicks, two thins and a thick."

The woman is not hip to the lingo of bar codes. She quickly edges away, giving me a look you'd give a fly walking across your cheeseburger.

The supermarket hums with a palpable energy this evening. White track lighting shimmers seductively over beckoning shelves and freezers. A Dire Straits tune, horribly mangled by Muzak, wafts softly from the overhead speakers. The meat section is alive with possibility as an old man rounds the aisle and... rams his cart into my knee.

I go down as if shot with a deer rifle. The boneless bottom round falls from my hand and skitters across the floor.

"Sorry," says the man.

"Oh, no prob..." I start to say, but he's already moving on, eyes riveted on a huge Ritz cracker display. My knee is throbbing violently.

Oh, there'll probably be the orthopedist to call. And x-rays to schedule. And maybe even a soft cast to get used to. But it's Friday night and a deranged old geezer with a runaway cart is not going to spoil my fun, no sir.

Somewhere, I know, Happy Hour is in full swing. Somewhere, there is music and laughter and fast-track junior executives devouring steaming plates of buffalo wings.

Somewhere, lovers giddy on wine coolers and imported beer grope at one another across a faux mahogany bar, minds racing ahead to the delicious possibility of furtive assignations in cheap motel rooms.

But here's where the *real* action is, folks: Scott Tissue, two for 96 cents. Lucerne shredded cheese, $1.89. Land 'O Lakes margarine, 49 cents. Bumble Bee tuna, 58 cents. Hires root beer ("Great Value!" says the happy face sign), 99 cents.

No, you can *have* your Happy Hour. You can *have* your Corona-and-lime crowd with their sticky hands poised over countless bowls of trail mix, enduring dreary "what's-your-sign?" conversations amid a thick haze of cigarette smoke.

Me, I'm right where I want to be. A social life in free fall? Don't you believe it. Even with a ruptured patella — I'm not a medical doctor, but that's what it feels like — I'm adrenalized here.

So much to see, so much to do. I limp over to a rack of lurid supermarket tabloids. The headline on one screams: "MOM'S TERRIFYING ORDEAL: A COYOTE ATE MY BABY!" Beautiful. If the dailies ran stuff like that, circulation would triple.

There is — God help me, but I love it — a certain anarchy about the supermarket. People leave their carts in the middle aisles and wander off in search of Lucky Leaf applesauce (regular and chunky) and Mazola corn oil.

People bump their carts into other carts, refusing to yield the right of way. Still, you can't have some crazy old coot plowing into people's *knees*, for God's sake. I have a good mind to call my attorney. Except it's Friday night and he's probably draped over the bar at Chi-Chi's, parachuting into another margarita.

I know. I've seen this man in action, chatting up 22-year-old English majors with rambling, semi-coherent harangues on the impact of Mark Twain. He'll be no good until Monday at the earliest.

Finally, my basket is full. It's time to go. The checkout counter is busy. The sign above me says "Express Lane — 9 items or less." So much for law and order. The glowering woman in front of me has 12 items in her cart. God knows what kind of arithmetic *she's* using. My guess: the old three-cans-of-peaches-count-as-one routine.

Still I grit my teeth and say nothing. With my luck, she's the wife of that deranged old man and, if I object, she'll club me over the head with a zucchini. Or she could be packing a piece in that raincoat and just *itching* to plug my one good kneecap. Isn't *every* lunatic armed these days?

I walk out into the night. The parking lot is teeming. Car horns are blaring. Great clouds of exhaust fumes swirl upward to the sky.

Shoppers hurry past me, their faces flushed with excitement. A woman tugs at her husband's elbow and squeals: "Mort! Those tortilla chips are on sale!"

He nods happily. You can almost smell the money burning a hole in his wallet.

I head home marveling.

You think this sort of stuff goes on in Cuba on Friday nights? Not a chance.

The Non-Renaissance Man

Useless as a whatchamacallit

When it comes to being handy, I can barely work a shower curtain, therefore qualifying as one of the growing numbers of mechanically impaired in this country.

We mechanically impaired ask only to be treated with the same basic dignity accorded other disadvantaged people.

Unfortunately, mechanical impairment (or "un-handiness") is a disability that's too long been ignored in our society.

There are no telethons featuring a weeping, exhausted Jerry Lewis, bow tie askew and perspiration streaming down his forehead, gently cradling a man who's fumbling badly with an adjustable wrench.

There are no support groups where the mechanically impaired gather to drink coffee and smoke cigarettes and share their feelings of inadequacy around a flex-head ratchet or bent-nose pliers.

In the words of one high school shop teacher in northern Virginia, the inability to work with one's hands or even engage a simple 5-horsepower air compressor (40 PSI, single-phase pump) represents "the last taboo" among adult males.

Nevertheless, the figures are indeed alarming. As of this writing, there are over 30 million mechanically impaired people in this country who can barely screw in a light bulb. Another 65 million are considered "functional dolts," which means they could possibly fix a leaky toilet, but only after watching a 45-minute videotape entitled "Home Repairs From A-to-Z."

The figures are also deceiving, however, since many of the mechanically impaired have yet to come out of the closet, for fear of being ridiculed and ostracized.

Instead, they lead lives of quiet desperation, paralyzed with fear that someone will casually ask them to "Change that typewriter ribbon for me, will ya?" or "Hand me a 3/8th-inch drill bit, like a good fella."

I myself came out of the closet at the age of 14. We were puttering around my father's workbench in the garage when I suddenly blurted: "Dad, I... I don't know *how* to use a power saw!"

The look on his face was one I will never forget. What was it I saw there? Revulsion? Or was it pity? Whatever it was, I felt so empty inside, even as he hurriedly cleared his throat and changed the conversation by asking: "So... how are things going in school?"

Over the years, I compensated for my inadequacy around power tools by becoming a writer, quietly building compound sentences instead of tool sheds, fashioning elaborate paragraphs instead of intricate wooden decks.

Is it all bleakness and despair for the mechanically impaired? Pretty much so, although there are one or two advantages to being un-handy, hard as that might be for normal people to visualize.

For one thing, people more or less leave you alone when something needs to be repaired. When something breaks around the house, my wife doesn't even *look* in my direction anymore. She just picks up the phone and calls the plumber or electrician or whomever, without making a big fuss over their $75-an-hour rates. She's really a terrific woman.

The neighbors don't bother you, either. They never interrupt you in the middle of "Cheers" to ask about fixing their sump pump. Tell you the truth, I don't even know what a sump pump is. (Two years ago, I probably wouldn't have admitted that. Therapy has certainly helped.)

Here is another advantage to being mechanically impaired: You never have to worry about people borrowing your tools and not returning them, mainly because you don't have *any* tools.

No, check that. Your average mechanically impaired person generally owns a hammer and a screwdriver. The regular kind of screwdriver, not that Phipps-head thing, or whatever you call it.

But nobody ever wants to borrow a hammer or screwdriver. They always want to borrow Craftsman torque wrenches and 7,500-watt portable generators and orbital-action sanders. That's why a typical exchange with my neighbors would go something like this:

"Say, you wouldn't have an 8-inch cast iron drill press, would you?"

"Uh, no, I wouldn't."

No wonder they used to think I was a pretty quiet guy, not much of a conversationalist.

The funny thing is, I used to lie about being handy when I was younger, when I wanted to be with the "in" crowd.

"Well," I'd say, "I *used* to have an 8-inch cast iron drill press. But I gave it to Goodwill."

Now I don't even bother making up stories. I've come to terms with my impairment, if not those $75-an-hour repair bills.

It's something I just have to live with.

Sorry, but that'll cost extra

The crisis began a few days ago when I sat down to watch TV and the screen began to go dim.

This I recognized as big trouble.

The moment the TV began to go dim, I had a vision.

In this vision, I could see an open window and a stack of $100 bills on a nearby table.

And as the vision unfolded, the $100 bills could be seen floating out the window.

They floated along on a gentle current of wind, eventually landing in a small shop owned by a fellow named Joe.

And now here was this Joe, putting these $100 bills in his pocket and handing me a piece of paper, which was some sort of receipt.

Joe appeared to be smiling. I appeared pale and shaken.

I knew what the vision meant. But instead of panicking, I mouthed a silent prayer and went to bed.

Maybe, I told myself, the TV would be better in the morning.

And maybe hell would freeze over, too.

The next day I nonetheless padded down to the family room and turned on the TV once again.

This time, there were even more distressing signs of troubles. In addition to the dimness, there were thin lines criss-crossing the screen.

The whole effect was as if you were watching "Good Morning America" from the Voyager II orbiting Mars.

So that day I called the TV repair shop and the phone was answered, ironically enough, by a fellow named Joe.

I explained the problem and, maybe it was my imagination, but I swore I heard laughter in the background.

Joe asked if I could bring the TV to his shop. I explained this would be impossible, as the TV was the size of a small building.

Joe said he would have to charge me extra for making a house call.

I said I understood. And as the words left my mouth, there came a new vision.

This time we were standing next to a bank vault, me and Joe and another man, whom I took to be Joe's helper.

Suddenly, the door to the vault flew open and here were all these $100 bills gushing forth from the vault like a green tornado.

And while I stood rooted to the ground in shock — for this apparently was *my* money blowing away — here were Joe and his helper scooping up the $100 bills and cackling hysterically.

In this vision, as in the previous one, I appeared to be pale and shaken. Which is how I went to bed that night.

So the next day a yellow van appeared in my driveway and a man with a tool kit jumped from the van and knocked on my door.

It was Joe. He seemed in terrific spirits, as if he'd recently had a good laugh.

"Can I get you a cup of coffee?" I said.

"Do you have decaffeinated?" he asked.

I apologized and said I did not.

Joe said he would have to charge me extra for not having decaffeinated coffee.

I said I understood. By now there were so many visions crowding my brain that I was feeling positively feverish and wondering if it were not a touch of malaria.

Mentally I made a note: Do not offer Joe lunch. For I knew if I did not have his favorite bread or cold cuts, Joe would have to charge me extra.

For the next two hours, Joe crouched in front of the TV and fiddled with this knob and that tube and this electronic gizmo.

Things seemed to be going extremely well. He was whistling a merry tune that I recognized as "We're in the Money" from a Broadway musical of long ago.

Suddenly, he climbed to his feet.

"I gotta take part of your TV back to the shop for repairs," he said. "I'll be back in the morning."

"Joe," I said. "I'm only guessing here. But will that cost me extra?"

Joe shook his head sadly and said, yes, that was right. He added that if I wanted a loaner TV for the night, well, that too would be extra.

I said I did not need a loaner, as I'd be spending the night researching the state law on debtors' rights.

So the next day the yellow van again appeared in the driveway, with Joe in even better spirits than the day before. The last time I saw such unrestrained glee, a mechanic named Earl was informing me that my car had transmission problems.

It took Joe ten minutes to put the set together, and suddenly you could watch "Good Morning America" without thinking that cataracts were forming in both eyes.

We celebrated with a glass of orange juice, Joe's favorite, I learned.

The bill should be paid off soon.

Joe claims to know a good loan shark.

Recalling terror in the grass

Sensing that I was in way too fine a mood and needing to get in touch with the customary gloom that surrounds me, I went out yesterday and inspected my lawn.

The lawn squats like a giant ugly toad on all four sides of the house.

It has more ruts and holes in it than the Ho Chi Minh Trail, circa 1968. And now, as spring comes grudgingly to the Mid-Atlantic region, my grass is a lovely shade of grayish brown, reminiscent of an abandoned strip-mining site in Appalachia.

Staring at the lawn and envisioning the work it would take to make this eyesore even *semi*-presentable, I became more and more depressed.

Finally, I couldn't take it anymore. So I went back inside and laid myself down in a dark room, for several hours staring up at the ceiling and wondering where it all went wrong.

There was a time — God help me, it seems so long ago now — when I was actually proud of the lawn.

Back then I nurtured the lawn. I spread fertilizer fervently. I planted grass seed religiously. I lugged around heavy bags of peat moss and distributed it generously to protect the new seedlings.

I went through enough weed killer to defoliate the eastern half of the U.S. — one whiff of the stuff would probably have killed you right there, paralyzing your brain stem. But I didn't care.

I was out of my mind. And *into* my lawn.

And one day I... well, I got a little carried away.

A man at the local nursery — an *evil* little man, I realize now — turned me on to this new fertilizer, which was said to produce amazing results.

So I bought a bag of the stuff and spread it on my lawn.

In retrospect, I should have sensed something was amiss.

The powder made a hissing sound as it hit the grass. Soon the entire lawn was shrouded in gaseous vapors, which blocked out the sun. Vultures circled overhead.

Overnight, while I slept the deep, contented sleep of a man who's toiled hard in the fields, the lawn turned an unearthly shade of yellow.

By the morning's first light, you needed a pair of Ray-Bans to look at the lawn.

Two hours later, shades were not enough. Even to *peek* at the lawn without permanent damage to your corneas, you needed a special purple filter recommended by NASA.

This, of course, did not go over well in the neighborhood.

Little children became frightened and lapsed into hysterical crying jags upon seeing the lawn.

Adult passers-by became agitated and reported feelings of dread and anxiety long after passing my house.

"Too much nitrogen," my neighbor Al told me one day.

"Beg pardon?" I said. The noise from the de-fogging machine I had rented was making it hard to hear.

"The fertilizer had too much nitrogen."

The fertilizer had too much nitrogen... boy, I wanted to smack him! And I probably would have, too, except all of a sudden I was feeling kind of queasy, apparently from the fumes rolling off the lawn.

The following spring, I looked in the Yellow Pages and dialed a lawn-care service.

The next day, a truck pulled up to the house. The truck had flowers and smiley faces and talking shrubs painted on its side panels.

Two officious-looking men got out, unraveled some hoses, and proceeded to spray the lawn with chemicals.

The men insisted these chemicals were not harmful to human life or dog life, and that there was no need for us to don Mylex suits, oxygen masks, and rubber boots in order to play a game of wiffleball in the back yard.

Of course, this is similar to what they said about Agent Orange 20 years ago. But as of this writing, neither my wife nor I have begun to glow in the dark, and the children are not mysteriously levitating towards the ceiling or using telepathic powers to hurl lamps at each other — at least not that I know of.

Anyway, the lawn service helped somewhat. But gazing out at the grass now, I see that we might want to try something new this spring.

One idea (I'm just thinking out loud here) is this: We blacktop the whole thing. Then we bring in some old washing machines, piles of snow tires, the rusted hulks of abandoned cars. Start a junk business. Try to make a few bucks.

Knowing the neighbors, they'd probably complain about *that*, too.

House chores kick off new football season

The day dawned exactly as I had hoped. Rain slanted down in great sheets and the sky was the dull color of dishwater, and of course this made me deliriously happy.

By 12:30, preparations were well under way. The TV was tuned to "The NFL on CBS" and the beer was chilling nicely. There were Cheez-its in one bowl and potato chips in another, and a bag of salt-free peanuts in case any health nuts should wander over.

And then I heard *the voice.*

"What do you think you're doing?" she said. It seemed clear enough to *me.* You see a man sitting in front of a TV, drinking a beer, snacking like Orson Welles, listening to Brent Musburger discuss a safety blitz as if he were Jonas Salk detailing the polio vaccine. This man is not about to grab a hammer and slap a redwood deck together.

"First day of the football season," I said cheerfully. "Eagles-Redskins. Big, big game."

"The hole in the driveway needs fixing," she said.

I pointed to the window. Outside, the rain continued to fall steadily. Even to the untrained eye, the wind had kicked up to what was surely gale force velocity.

"I cannot go out there," I said. "They lost Amelia Earhart on a day like this."

Soon, a golden silence filled the room. On the TV, Brent said something to Jimmy the Greek. The two of then quaked with laughter. The Redskins took the field.

The Cheez-its had never tasted better. And suddenly I was struck with this thought: It was going to be a wonderful season.

It was about a half-hour later that I noticed the weather conditions had worsened dramatically.

The rain had stopped. Even more alarming, the sky was brightening, and the angry storm clouds of a short while ago were fleeing to the south.

I sensed another presence in the room immediately.

"It has stopped raining," she announced. "The sky is brightening."

"But it's damp out there," I said. "I could catch cold. If you happen by the Cheez-its, please, could I get a refill?"

Soon, a golden silence filled the room once more. On the TV, one of the Redskins was being carried off the field on a stretcher. It's a demanding game, pro football. One minute you seem the picture of health, the next a linebacker is snapping your leg back like a sapling in a hurricane.

As the fresh Cheez-its had not yet arrived and showed no signs of doing so, I shuffled off to the kitchen.

It has been this way since the beginning of time, I thought. You say no, the hole in the driveway will have to wait, and you become a non-person. You become just another nameless, faceless wretch who must fend for his own Cheez-its.

It was well into the third quarter when the phone rang.

It rang once and then twice and then many, many times, a loud, piercing, annoying ring. So it had come to this: a calculated form of harassment. Not only would she ignore a simple, plaintive request for more Cheez-its, she would not answer the phone.

The Eagles were driving, inside the 20. I picked up the phone. The voice on the other end sounded oddly familiar, despite the din created by the sellout crowd at RFK Stadium.

"You never call me anymore," said the voice. "You *could* call your own mother."

"The Eagles are on the 15," I said.

"Well, everything's fine here," said the voice. "Your sister was here the other day and ..."

Cunningham, the Eagles' quarterback, had taken the snap from center now. He rolled right, long legs chewing up the turf. But the Redskin defense was attacking in waves. Cunningham seemed properly rattled. He let the ball fly in the general direction of the Washington Monument.

Incomplete pass. I told the caller I would get back to her.

By now, it had become painfully clear that there would be little peace on this first day of the new football season.

In addition, the weather had become positively sickening: blue skies, sunshine, temperature creeping up into the high 80s.

I turned off the TV, permitted myself one final Cheez-it, and wandered out into the driveway.

There, I came upon a hole the size of a lunar crater.

Someone should really fix this thing, I thought.

But not today. You could really hurt yourself working in this heat.

There's a mouse in the house

The mood has been rather tense around our house lately with the discovery that there's a mouse the size of a golden retriever living in the kitchen.

This first came to my attention a week ago, when I walked into the house bone-tired after another long day of journalism.

People think newspaper writers don't get tired taking cheap shots at people and dealing in vicious innuendo and outrageous hyperbole, but believe me, we do. I'm not saying it's like swinging a pick in a coal mine, but still...

Anyway, I came home that day and found my wife nervously pacing the kitchen.

"There's a mouse in the house," she said quietly.

I thought it odd that she was speaking in rhyme, but the woman *has* been under a great deal of stress lately.

There was the strain of Christmas shopping and then all three children caught the flu. The poetry, I assumed, was a sign that she was about to snap. Judy Garland, at the inception of her first breakdown, was found huddled under a blanket, quoting Yeats. Or so I hear.

It's a little-known fact, but same thing with these poor people who suffer from post-traumatic stress disorder. Eight out of ten spend their days reciting passages from the works of Robert Frost.

In this case, however, there really *was* a mouse in the house. Silently, my wife showed me the evidence: nibbled food supplies, mouse droppings, the works.

So that evening, I went to the hardware store to buy something to get rid of this mouse.

I was thinking along the lines of a stun gun or some sort of chemical agent you could spray in the mouse's face. Mace maybe. But the clerk, a quiet man who'd been busy throwing stones at the pigeons on the sidewalk, suggested an old-fashioned mouse trap.

"You put the bait here, see," he said, his eyes lighting up, "then you pull this spring back, and when he steps over here — WHAMO! HA, HA, HA, HA!"

Hoo, boy. The man, I thought, was just a tad too enthusiastic for this line of work. He would have made a good football coach, though.

Anyway, that night I dutifully put the trap out and baited it with cheese. The next morning I ran downstairs and made an amazing discovery: The trap was still there — unsprung. But the cheese was *gone!* So right away, you know you're not dealing with a stupid mouse.

In fact, it seems to me that if a mouse is smart enough to steal the cheese from a trap, you ought to leave him alone. You don't want to antagonize a mouse like that. If you give him too much grief, he's probably smart enough to creep into your bedroom with a can of gasoline, soak the place up, and light a match.

But my wife didn't see it that way. The woman gets very jittery in the presence of rodents. She insisted that we bait the trap again, which I did.

The next morning I ran downstairs and made an even more amazing discovery. This time, not only was the cheese gone, *but so was the entire trap!*

Well, I had never seen anything like it. The way I envisioned it, we were dealing with a tough, savvy mouse, possibly all bulked up on steroids, who was laughing himself silly at our efforts to catch him.

"We're outta here," I told my wife. "Get the 'For Sale' sign out. Any mouse that cunning and aggressive must be built along the lines of a wolverine."

You talk about the intimidation factor. Apparently, here was a mouse with the presence of mind to stumble onto a trap in the dead of night and sneer: "Heh, heh, heh. Watch me *really* freak this guy out. I'll take the whole damn trap this time."

When I returned to the hardware store to buy another trap, I found the same clerk. This time he was poking at a cat with a curtain rod. Hold onto your hat, I said, but you know that mouse I've been chasing? He walked away with the trap!

"Oh yeah, that happens all the time," the clerk said.

It does?

"The mouse gets its tail or part of its leg caught in the trap and just keeps going."

Swell. But my God, the mouse must be the size of a palomino to do that!

"It could be a good-sized mouse. Here, kitty, kitty, kitty..."

So that's where we stand as of this writing. The mouse is still in the house. Sometimes we hear him late at night, draining six-packs of beer and cranking up his little stereo and laughing until he hurts.

Unless, of course, that's just the garbage disposal we're hearing.

Dear guys: here we come

In the mail the other day came a Christmas card from Don and Marie, along with a letter reporting that their oldest daughter Jessica (a prune-faced little brat when we knew her) has been accepted at Dartmouth.

The letter went on to enumerate the other "wonderful events!" the family celebrated in 1993.

It seems that Don was recently promoted and now makes such an incredible salary that they have to take their money to the bank in big Hefty trash bags.

Marie is doing well at her law firm, was named president of the Garden Club and PTA, and still managed to find time to grow a 200-pound, bell-shaped squash that took first place in its division at the state fair.

Their youngest, Alan, led his soccer team in scoring and is doing college-level physics in ninth grade as part of some super-mutant-gifted-and-talented program where, in their spare time, the students sit around and design shuttle re-entry systems for NASA.

The letter concludes, "Write back soon and tell us how things are with you!"

So I ripped a sheet of loose-leaf paper from one of the kids' school binders and moistened the tip of a No. 2 pencil and wrote:

Dear Don and Marie,

Please forgive the sloppy handwriting, but as I write this, the house is pitched at a 15-degree angle and my desk keeps rolling across the room, which I will explain in a moment.

All is well here. The kids are doing fine, too, I suppose. We don't see them much — they spend a lot of time watching TV in the basement. There is a sullenness about them, although maybe that's not surprising, given what happened to the house.

It started when we were moving some snow tires out to the front yard. That's where we keep the old refrigerators and washing machines. Suddenly, there was a noise like a rifle shot.

I ran to the back of the house and discovered a huge crack in the foundation. Within seconds, the house was tilting at a severe angle and the cable went out. Naturally, the kids went nuts, storming out of the basement and screaming: "This better be fixed in time for 'Ren and Stimpy'!"

We had to get a structural engineer out. He said it looks like the whole damn house is sinking. He also said it would cost big bucks to right it and reinforce the foundation.

Well, thank you very much, I thought. So much for Christmas presents this year.

The other night, as usual, we ate our dinner off tray tables in the living room, but it sure felt weird not to be watching "Wheel of Fortune."

Nancy suggested that we could have a conversation for a change. "About what?" the kids snarled.

"Well," she said, turning to me, "how's work going?"

"Don't ask," I said, poking my fork listlessly into a can of Dinty Moore stew. "Newspapers are on life-support systems. Long hours, little pay. End of story."

Nobody felt like eating after that. Then all of a sudden — because of the angle of the room, I guess — the TV slipped off its stand and started sliding down the hallway, whereupon the kids started whooping and chasing it. So that pretty much ended the conversation.

Let's see... what else? Well, Goldie's not around anymore. The little fella got hit by a mail truck a couple of days ago.

The kids were pretty torn up about it. Me, I never cared much for dogs, and even less for Goldie. He didn't know very many tricks except "sit," and what dog doesn't know that?

Anyway, we buried Goldie out back under one of the pink flamingo lawn ornaments. It was a very moving ceremony, although right in the middle of the prayers, with everyone bawling and stuff, Sean said: "When will the cable come back on?"

"It wouldn't kill you to read a book," I said.

The kids all looked at each other and smirked, and then little Chrissie said: "Heck, we might as well finish planting Goldie."

I said I didn't know when the cable would be back, that these things take time. With the house listing at a 15-degree angle, it seems to me we're lucky even to have electricity and running water.

Now all the kids do day after day is stay down in the basement and play Nintendo.

I thought I smelled something burning down there. Like soup or franks and beans or something. You don't think they have a hotplate down there, do you?

Love to all,
Kevin, Nancy and the kids

P.S. Let us know when we can come and visit!

Telephone is my hang up

Legend has it that the moment Alexander Graham Bell invented the telephone, his mother called and said: "How come you never call me?"

Bell managed to stammer some feeble excuse about work piling up in the lab, but his mom would have none of it.

She made him feel so guilty that Bell considered dropping his patent application, apparently preferring that someone else take the blame for the havoc he had unleashed with his new invention.

It also caused Bell to ignore his mother for the rest of his life, insisting to everyone that he was raised by gorillas.

More than 100 years later, we are still bedeviled by the telephone. I am bedeviled by it more than anyone. Therefore, I have compiled the following rules of telephone etiquette:

RULE NO. 1: LITTLE KIDS SHOULD BE SEEN AND NOT HEARD.

The minute a little kid answers the phone, the receiver should be snatched from his or her little hands by an adult. I am even drawing up a bill mandating that a 5,000-volt electrical charge be sent through the receiver if used by anyone under the age of five, although I'm sure certain namby-pamby members of Congress will balk at such an innovative technique.

The alternative, however, are hellish conversations such as this:
Little kid: "Hu-wo?"
You: "Hi, Bobby, it's Uncle Kevin. Is your daddy home?"
Little kid: "Uncle Kevin's not here."
You: "Ha, ha. No, *this* is Uncle Kevin. Let me speak to your dad."
Little kid: "I can count to ten. Want to hear? One, two, three..."
You: "Get your dad, please,or Uncle Kevin will feed you to the alligators."
Little kid: "...four, five, six..."
You: "Bobby, do you like toys? If you get your daddy, Uncle Kevin will..."
Little kid: "Bye-bye!" *(Click.)*
And they wonder why Uncle Kevin drinks.

RULE NO. 2: IT HELPS WHEN YOU SPEAK INTO THE MOUTHPIECE.

I don't want to get bogged down with a lot of technical mumbo-jumbo here, but the mouthpiece is that part of the telephone closest to your lips.

Still too heavy? OK, when Mr. Sound is channeled directly into Mr. Mouthpiece, it is more clearly detected by Mr. Ear.

This makes for a more pleasant conversation between you, Mr. or Ms. Inconsiderate, and me, Mr. Person With the Short Fuse.

I try to explain this to my mother whenever she calls to tell me I never call.

The reason I never call is that I can barely hear her. It sounds as if I'm talking to someone in the Falkland Islands.

No, I take that back. It sounds like I'm talking to the space shuttle Discovery as it makes its way through an asteroid belt.

When I tell her this, she always says: "We must have a bad connection."

Meanwhile, the mouthpiece is either tucked under her chin, or is up around her eyes. This partly explains why, under place of birth, I now write: Unknown wolf's den, Appalachian foothills.

RULE NO. 3: DON'T WAKE ME.

You know how, when you call someone and they sound groggy and disoriented, they always insist that no, you didn't wake them up? Well, I'm not like that. When you wake *me*, you'll know you didn't dial a seminary.

In fact, here's a snappy comeback you can use if you happen to get one of those unsolicited wake-up calls:

Caller: "Did I wake you?"

You: "No, I had to get up anyway to answer the phone."

Then send some hard-looking guys over to that person's house to throw him down the stairs.

RULE NO. 4: GET TO THE POINT OR I'M HANGING UP.
The other day, I received an unsolicited call from a local pizza merchant. The conversation went like this:
Pizza guy: "How are you today?"
Me: "I was doing fine until this shampoo got in my eyes."
Pizza guy: "Good, good. Sir, do you like pizza?"
Me: "Gee, I don't know, let me check my high school yearbook. Likes: football, '67 Mustangs and the Rolling Stones. Dislikes: rainy days, geometry and phony people. Nope, nothing about pizza."
It took the pizza guy another two minutes to say they were opening a new store near my house.
I told him this was quite a surprise to me, as I was opening a McDonald's on that very corner. I thought I heard the phone drop.
RULE NO. 5: NO CONVERSATION SHOULD LAST MORE THAN THREE MINUTES.
If you can't say it in three minutes, write a letter. That's what Mom does now.
There's only one problem, though. She wants to know how come I never *write back*.

A special kind of tuneup

My friend Artie the car mechanic was having some trouble with a letter he was writing and, knowing that I was in the writing business, asked me to take a look at it.

"Don't know when I'll get to it," I said. "I'm pretty backed up. Got an essay that needs body work, two columns that need polishing, and a Noriega satire that needs a complete overhaul."

He seemed disappointed with this news. I hate disappointing my customers, but this time of year, everyone's correspondence seems to break down at once.

"What sort of trouble is your letter giving you?" I asked.

"It's hard to describe," he said. "It just sort of sits there. There's no zip to it, no pep. You get to the middle and it just dies out."

From what he was telling me, it sure didn't sound good — not that I was going to make a snap diagnosis over the phone.

"It could be something simple like a sentence that needs tightening," I said. "Then again, it could be blown syntax and need a major restructuring of paragraphs. There's no way to tell until I get it up on the word processor."

"When will that be?" he asked anxiously.

"Hard to know," I said. "Could be tomorrow, could be the next day. Bring it in and we'll have a look."

He dropped the letter off at my shop early the next morning, but I was up to my fingertips in a Leona Helmsley lampoon and barely had time to say hello.

Once I got Artie's letter up on the word processor, hell, it was easy to spot the problem.

For one thing, the prose immediately after the salutation was haggard and worn and had to be replaced.

The middle of the text was OK — he was telling his mom about his recent vacation — but there were twisted metaphors all over the place and the tail end of the account was swollen and disjointed.

No wonder the damn thing seemed sluggish and listless.

Personally, I was surprised it even made a dozen paragraphs before conking out.

Artie called back around two that afternoon. I wiped the ink from my hands with an 8-by-11 sheet of bond paper and grabbed the phone.

"Arturo my man, got some bad news for you," I said. "You're gonna have to leave it here for a few days. The lead is shot and it needs a new adjective or two where you describe your visit to Disney World.

"Besides, I gotta order some parts. That could take a while."

"*Parts?*" he said.

"Artie," I growled, "you ever change the ribbon on your typewriter?"

"Well, I... I keep meaning to do it," he said. "But you know how it is. A guy forgets."

"You're supposed to change those things every 3,000 words," I said. "Your ribbon was filthy. That's why it kept smudging the 'g' and 'm' keys and you can't make out that part about Mickey and Goofy leading the parade."

I'll tell you, numbskulls like Artie never cease to amaze me.

They go out and buy a brand new Smith-Corona or Underwood — they don't care about the sticker price — and the thing is loaded with options such as automatic carriage return, a built-in dictionary, letter- and word-correction keys.

And then they don't take care of it.

My philosophy is simple. Either pay me now or pay me later.

If you don't want to plunk down $3.98 for a new typewriter ribbon, fine. Be that way. It's no skin off my nose.

Just don't come crying to me when you bang out "Dear Mom" and the letters fade so badly it's like you're reading it from a jetliner at 30,000 feet.

Anyway, Artie was understandably upset that he had to leave his letter in the shop for a few days, but there was nothing I could do about it.

"Call me Thursday," I said. "There's an Olivetti dealer up in Philly who owes me a favor. If he ships that ribbon right away and I get around to fixing your grammar and punctuation, you can pick it up that day."

To make a long story short, we finally took care of Artie.

To tide him over for a few days, I lent him an old letter of mine — it was a '72 note I had dashed off to my mother when I was in college.

Sure, it wasn't one of Hemingway's dispatches from Paris, but it did the job. Artie's mom never knew the difference, apparently assuming her son had suffered some sort of mid-life crisis and was now taking in beer blasts at a small liberal arts school in New Jersey.

I had to charge Artie an arm and a leg, but what do you expect for that kind of service?

Parts, labor, it all adds up.

Letter writing is a lost art

I'll tell you what we as Americans don't do enough of anymore: we don't write enough letters.

You know how it is. You've been meaning to sit down and dash off a note to your annoying ne'er-do-well cousin in Minnesota.

But then you get to watching, say, MTV and it's the usual video parade of saucy vixens in leather and chains, or skimpy negligees, or shimmering bustiers, sleek fishnet stockings tracing the soft outline of flesh as they...

Anyway, before you know it, the evening's shot and you're staring at a piece of personalized stationery with nothing to show for your efforts except the salutation "Dear Earl."

This is why professional writing instructors recommend you write in a brightly lit and well-ventilated setting, preferably one that does not include cable.

The first order of business is to decide what tone you're looking for in your letter.

Bemused? Didactic? Self-effacing? Seriously disturbed? Whatever your decision, this is the tone you'll want to adopt consistently as you compose a letter that is both informative and entertaining.

A good way to open a letter is with an apology of some sort. As we are all, let's face it, scum on this Earth, there's always something to apologize for, whether it's the tardiness of your letter or your recent embezzlement of $500,000 of company funds.

Keep your apology breezy and to the point, then move on. ("Please forgive the poor penmanship, but off in the distance I can hear the baying of the hounds and now there's a police helicopter overhead, its searchlight piercing through the dense underbrush. How are mother and the children?")

One note of caution: It is usually considered bad form to begin a letter with disturbing news.

For instance, if Uncle Harry was in a bus that plunged over a cliff and tumbled 300 feet down a steep ravine, igniting into a wall of flames, it's probably best to save this bulletin for the sixth or seventh paragraph.

I myself would try to work it in while perhaps passing on a favorite recipe. ("...and line a 9-inch pie plate with graham cracker crust. Beat 6 egg yolks. Add 1 cup lime juice. By the way, did you hear about poor Uncle Harry? The bus company informs us the driver was one of their best, an alert and capable fellow never known to touch a drop of alcohol until his wife walked out on him for a stock car driver. Wasn't that always Uncle Harry's luck?")

This next bit of advice is important: Don't be afraid to make things up.

It's no sin to arrive at a lull in your letter ("Aunt Betty is fine, although coughing up an alarming amount of phlegm") and then suddenly begin to detail a terrible fire down at the nursing home and your heroic single-handed rescue of 11 senior citizens — two of whom were blind.

Remember, you're not under oath here and, again, you do want to be informative and entertaining. And what could be more entertaining than a taut narrative about a towering five-alarm blaze and one man's selfless determination to save lives by crawling along a burning ledge over and over again with a frightened elderly person slung around his neck?

One of the best letters I ever received was from an old high school buddy detailing his Peace Corps stint in the high Andes Mountains of Ecuador.

It was a very moving account of a hardscrabble life among the Mestizo Indians and their gritty struggles to overcome poverty and sickness while eking out a living raising cocoa and coffee.

I later came to find out the fellow was actually working as the assistant night manager at a Rite-Aid in New Jersey and playing in a modified slo-pitch softball league for Bucky's Tavern on Mondays and Thursdays.

Nevertheless, I was overcome by the sheer passion of his prose. And I had no doubt that, if he ever decided to give up stocking the shelves with Mylanta and straightening the magazine rack and setting up the Hallmark card displays, he would have done a bang-up job in volunteer work.

Perhaps the single question that is most asked by letter writers is: How do I end my letter gracefully?

Nothing is worse than a letter that overstays its welcome. If you have nothing else to say, don't say it.

Instead, bring your narrative to a swift conclusion and sign off, as in the following:

"Finally, I must tell you that the bull-headed skinflints who run this town have closed our local chapter of the Sweet Adelines. My life is so empty now. I sit here consumed with the thought of swallowing a fistful of pills and taking a hammer to Raymond's head as he lays sleeping peacefully on the couch. My best to you and your family."

Don't forget your return address and a cheery stamp.

The readers strike back

The problem with writing a column is that you get a lot of mail, much of it scrawled in crayon, which you are nonetheless expected to answer.

As a matter of personal preference, I like letters such as this:

"Dear Sir,

"You are a very funny writer, and the only reason I buy the local fish wrap. That column you wrote about all TV repairmen being crooks was a *hoot*! If you're ever in Monroe, N.Y., give me a call and Erma and I will treat you to a fine dinner at the Goose Pond Inn.

"Your No. 1 fan,

"Earl T. Longsworthy, Jr.

"P.S.: My brother-in-law Pete runs the local Jiffy Lube. Maybe we can see about a free 14-point service check for your car, too!"

Obviously, a letter as gracious as this deserves a prompt and pleasant response:

"Dear Earl,

"Thank you for your very nice letter. As it happens, I will be in the Monroe area on... well, when is good for you? Your generous offer of dinner is most appreciated — a quick phone call to the Goose Pond confirmed that Thursday is 'Steak and Lobster' night, so perhaps we should circle that day on our calendars.

"Also, does the free 14-point service check include transmission fluid?

"By all means, let's get together!

"P.S.: Tell your lovely wife Erma I said hello! And Pete, too!

"P.S. #2: By any chance, would Pete have a spare fan belt for an '87 Subaru station wagon?"

Unfortunately, much of the mail also comes from psychos — a psycho being defined as anyone who disagrees with the columnist:

"Dear Sir,

"In a recent column, you likened accordion music to the sound made by a dying animal in a fur trap, and said it induces in the average listener feelings of nausea and revulsion.

"You also stated that accordion players lead empty, meaningless lives filled with prolonged bouts of self-loathing and drug abuse.

"I respectfully disagree.

"Thomas N.O. Waznewski

"(A former polka band member!)"

This type of sick, threatening letter also demands a swift response:

"Dear Mr. Waznewski,

"Your ranting screed reached my desk this a.m. If you persist in this kind of harassment, I will have no choice but to call the police.

"P.S. I urge you, for your own sake and the sake of your family, to seek counseling for the anger eating away at you."

A columnist also gets a good deal of mail from nit-pickers, who delight in pointing out tiny factual errors:

"Dear Sir,

"In your column about mimes, in which you call them 'boring, despicable creatures,' you stated that the great Marcel Marceau 'blew his brains out in a lonely Paris cafe, no doubt guilt-ridden over the suffering he had caused so many.'

"This is to inform you that Marcel Marceau is very much alive.

"Marian Anderson."

Here, a short snappy reply is really all that is necessary.

"Dear Ms. Anderson,

"People like you make me sick.

"P.S. — I urge you to talk to a therapist about your anger."

Much of a columnist's mail consists of letters from PR people trying to get you to do a story on their client or cause:

"Dear Columnist,

"Michael DeVoy was trapped in an elevator for 57 days when his office building was hastily quarantined for Legionnaires Disease and the power shut off — a move Michael's supervisor neglected to tell him was imminent. Hours after he was finally freed, Michael fell 50 feet into a well, where he remained for another three weeks, living on rain water and the occasional centipede that happened by.

"Now this remarkable man has written a book about his ordeal called: *Hello? Can Anyone Hear Me?* The author will be in your area soon and will be available for interviews.

"The Collins Agency, New York City."

Even if the letter does not pique the columnist's interest, it deserves a reply:

"Dear Sirs,

"While Mr. DeVoy's story is certainly compelling, I'm afraid I'll have to pass. This is a sunny, upbeat, slice-of-life column. The negative tone of Mr. DeVoy's experiences would be too jarring for my readers.

"Thanks anyway,"

"P.S. — I myself am writing a book about a disgruntled, cocaine-addicted accordion enthusiast who harasses and stalks a crusading, idealistic newspaper columnist. *Any interest?*"

O.D.ing on
Holidays

Pasteurizing oneself in '94

Nineteen ninety-four is going to be my year, yes sir, and already I am unlocking my Inner Child and empowering myself through a program of meditation, visualization and other neat things most people couldn't *begin* to understand.

There will be so many changes in me, it'll make your head spin.

For openers, I'm starting a new exercise program, a kind of ultra-Nautilus thing. I'm shooting for a 32-inch waist and 68-inch chest — by May. My wife says that's ridiculous. We'll see.

They laughed at Louis Pasteur, too. Louis Pasteur didn't lift weights, but he talked about the role of micro-organisms in fermentation and the people in 19th century France thought he was nuts.

Or he'd hold up a test tube and muse: "Perhaps disease is spread by living germs, such as bacteria," and his lab assistants would roll their eyes and make tiny circles around their temples with their forefingers.

But Pasteur didn't care what people thought. I don't either. Go ahead and laugh. It'll just make me more of a madman in the gym. You watch, in four months I'll be able to bench-press a Buick.

Let's see... what else? I resolve to cut out the fat in my diet. Not *some* fat, but *all* fat. I will eat nothing but fruits and vegetables, along with wild grains, roots, etc., all of which I'll wash down with natural spring water.

The next time you see me, I'll have the body fat of a greyhound to go along with my newly sculpted physique, which again is just around the corner. I'll bet you wish you had my kind of discipline and resolve, but you don't, so don't even *try* getting into that kind of shape.

I also promise to improve my mind as well as my body in '94. I'm going to re-read the classics: *Moby Dick, Anna Karenina*, you name it, one per week. Or maybe one every three days, if it's not too thick.

It's funny, four days ago I was reading a *People* profile on Luke Perry; now I'm devouring Joyce's *Ulysses*. Well, maybe devouring isn't the word. Quite frankly, though, my IQ has probably risen 30, 40 points already.

Here's one I bet you don't think I can keep (but I can): I promise to never again scream at my kids. Ever.

When the 11-year-old gets the 8-year old in a headlock in the back of the car, and she starts screaming like someone just hacked off her arm and he yells "Well she *started* it!" and my wife, who is driving, turns around momentarily, allowing the car to veer into the path of a road construction crew, I will remain calm.

"Kids, kids, kids," I'll say, "Can't we all get along? How 'bout we pull into the next rest stop and talk it over?"

Emotionally, I will be a rock in '94.

When someone cuts me off on the expressway, instead of slamming the steering wheel and sticking my head out the window and screaming: "I HOPE YOU ROT IN HELL, YOU MISERABLE PIG!" and then leaning on the horn and flashing my lights and tailgating him for miles at speeds in excess of 75 mph until that final, violent confrontation with a tire iron on the exit ramp, I'll just take a deep breath and say: "That's OK. We're all brothers. You have a nice day, hear?"

From now on, I will practice one random act of kindness per day, depending on the weather. Maybe I'll go over to old man Withers' house after the next snowfall and shovel his driveway.

(This is probably neither here nor there, but you wonder why he couldn't shovel it himself. It's not like his arms are broken or anything. Plus the guy is a retired stockbroker — he could pay some kid to clear his walkway. But... whatever.)

In '94, I promise to make time for myself. When I come home from work each day, I'll slip into a room with a sturdy lock on the door, something with a deadbolt, or even a time-release mechanism.

Then, when the kids start pounding on the door and screaming: "I need help with my math homework!" or my wife yells "You have to run to the store for me!" I'll smile and crank up Tom Petty and the Heartbreakers until it drowns out their pathetic voices.

Ironically, if you take away the CD player, this is very similar to what Louis Pasteur used to do. People think that, given his tremendous accomplishments, Pasteur was all go, go, go.

They figure he was stuck behind those beakers and test tubes 18 hours a day, never relaxing except when he'd take in the occasional public beheading, witch burning or affair of that nature in his blood-stained lab coat.

But the truth is, Pasteur would often find a quiet place and pour himself a glass of wine and shut out the rest of the world, if only for a few minutes.

I don't know where I picked that little factoid up. Did I read it, or did somebody mention it to me? I forget.

But it doesn't matter. I've promised myself not to get hung up on details anymore.

Toughing it out on Turkey Day

I'll never forget the wonderful Thanksgiving of '61, when we all
jumped in the car for the trip to Aunt Pat's and Dad backed down the
driveway smack into a blue Plymouth.

"Dammit, Bill," my mom said, but Dad was already out the car,
jawing at the other driver, who turned out to be an off-duty cop.

Our rear bumper was caved in pretty bad. Dad was plenty
steamed and didn't say a word all the way to Chappaqua. We sat in
traffic for an hour on the bridge while he drummed his fingers
furiously on the dashboard. You could almost *see* the smoke pouring
out his ears.

When we finally got to Aunt Pat's, the adults gathered around the
kitchen table and the kids ran outside to play on the swings. About
five minutes later, my cousin Bernadette let go of the swing and it
caught my younger brother Stephen on the bridge of the nose.

Well, there was blood spurting out all over the place, and, sure
enough, the little baby started screaming. Everyone in the house ran
outside and my aunt yelled to my father: "Bill, you better run him up
to the emergency room, see if he needs stitches!"

They came back an hour and a half later. Dad collapsed into a
chair and said: "What the hell *else* can go wrong?"

Then he downed three glasses of wine in about five minutes and
lit a cigarette. His hands were shaking badly.

Finally we sat down to dinner. The turkey and stuffing and sweet
potatoes were delicious, although by this point we were all waiting for
someone to start choking violently on a bone or something.

After dinner, we were all stuffed and people started lumbering
into the living room. There was a football game on TV, the Detroit
Lions against somebody, I think. It was about 110 degrees in the
house and you couldn't open any of the windows — they were nailed
shut on account of my aunt's asthma.

Anyway, one by one, people began to nod off. Finally the only
ones awake were me and Uncle Mike, who felt compelled to start a
conversation.

"So, you're in fifth grade, eh?" he said.

"What's the *point* of school, anyway?" I said. "All you do is listen to all these stupid teachers talk about stupid stuff you'll never need in life. Like who cares about the Lewis and Clark Expedition?"

He didn't say anything after that. Then pretty soon he was pulling a quilt around himself and he dropped off, too.

Well, I wasn't going to sit there by myself watching football. The other kids were outside, but I decided to go upstairs and find my cousin Willie's *Playboys*.

I didn't know where he hid them, so I searched under his bed and behind the bookshelf. Finally I found them way back in his closet. But when I grabbed one and stood up, I slammed my forehead against a coat hook and raised a knot the size of a tangerine over one eye.

I was so woozy I thought I was going to black out right there, but I managed to stumble back downstairs.

The football game was almost over, not that anybody cared at this point. I certainly didn't, not with blurred vision and a possible concussion.

About an hour later, everyone in the living room began stirring. Finally my aunt yawned and stretched and wiped this little stream of drool from her chin with a Kleenex.

"Anybody hungry?!" she chirped.

So we all lumbered into the kitchen for more turkey and another slice of mince pie, which was exactly what we needed at that point. If you listened closely, you could actually *hear* arteries clogging. I thought we might have someone keel over into a plate right there.

Finally Dad started looking at his watch, which was a hint for Mom to say: "Well, I guess we better be going..."

So we said thanks and good-bye, and piled into the car for the ride home. My old man was still half-lit from the wine, you could tell that. After he'd driven a couple blocks and nearly sheared off three mailboxes, Mom made him pull over so she could drive.

The rest of the ride was a nightmare. It was rainy and foggy on the expressway and these huge trucks kept roaring up behind us and flashing their lights, mainly because Mom was doing 35 miles an hour in the center lane.

"For crissakes, Noreen, give it some gas!" Dad shouted.

Which was when Mom started crying. My head was pounding and I thought I was going to be sick. We missed our exit on the Thruway and had to go all the way up to Kingston and double back.

Pulling into the driveway, Mom got a little too close to the elm tree and the car's antenna snapped off.

I ran inside and took a couple of Alka Seltzers and went to bed. Memories like these, they last a lifetime.

Please, no more socks or combs

The thing that should be stressed up front is that I don't presume to speak for *all* fathers here.

But let me say this: on Father's Day, many of us would prefer to be remembered in ways that do *not* involve a Greek fisherman's cap or ceramic coffee mug bearing the inscription: "World's Greatest Dad."

We have also had it up to here — I'm holding my hand at chin level now — with bathrobes, especially the silken kind that cause the wearer to eerily resemble Ricky Ricardo lounging between sets at the Copa.

Unfortunately, though, the typical Father's Day scenario too often degenerates into something like this:

The beaming family gathers around Dad at the kitchen table.

Mom nods her head and one of the little dears hands Dad a sappy Father's Day card. Another little dear hands him a carefully wrapped package.

Dad spends the requisite three seconds reading aloud from the card's swollen prose ("Because you are so special to us, blah, blah, blah") and tosses the card over his shoulder.

Now he tears into the gift. And within seconds the smile fades from his face, replaced by a look of... well, *disquietude* is not far off the mark.

"Oh," Dad says. There's a long pause and then: "It's a... a pair of socks." Another pause. "Navy blue socks. And what are these here? *Brown* socks."

Feeling enormously pleased with themselves, the other family members clap Dad on the back and go off to various activities.

Dad, on the other hand, quietly shuffles off to his bedroom, where he will sit with the shades drawn, staring intently at the dead moth on the ceiling and wondering where it all went awry.

Of course, fathers, by and large, are used to such rejection.

We live with it every day. And it's never more acutely felt than when we compare the hoopla surrounding Mother's Day to the quiet outbreak of yawning that accompanies Father's Day.

Mothers, on *their* day, are traditionally remembered with breakfast in bed, candy, flowers, romantic weekend getaways, jewelry, I could go on.

A father, on the other hand, will be lucky to receive a pair of bedroom slippers — further adding to his sense that as far as sleepwear is concerned, he's now in lock-step with not only Ricky Ricardo, but Fred Mertz as well.

If a father is particularly blessed, he'll be informed by his wife that, since it's Father's Day, he will not be required to take out the garbage. One of the kids will do it instead.

Bitter? Oh, I don't know... bitter isn't the right word for it.

Hurt. There you go. And empty.

One year — this is a true story — I received a comb for Father's Day.

Now maybe you're thinking: OK, a comb. But it was probably a real *neat* comb, huh? Maybe one of those tortoise-shell jobs with silver inlay that comes with...

Nope. It was a black comb. A cheap black comb. You know those plastic tubs full of combs that you see in drug stores with a cardboard sign saying 49 cents each?

That's the kind of comb we're talking about here.

The comb was a gift from a relative. I don't want to mention her name. Let's just say it was my wife's side of the family, and leave it at that.

Anyway, when my mother-in-law... excuse me, when this *person* handed me what appeared to be a very tiny gift on Father's Day, obviously I wasn't expecting a CD player.

But a *comb?!*

"You needed a comb," my wife said later.

Well, yeah. I also needed some toothpaste, but that probably wouldn't make a swell gift, either.

You talk about bitter. This is the kind of thing that causes some men to slip into battle fatigues, dab some boot-black under their eyes, and head onto a highway overpass with a rifle.

Now maybe this next point borders on nit-picking, but here goes.

While a lot of fathers are handy around the house and appreciate a Craftsman variable speed reversible drill, many of us can barely work a shower curtain.

For those fathers who are mechanically impaired, a 10-inch electronic radial saw with digital readout might *look* impressive, but will ultimately find use only as a doorstop.

Now perhaps the harried gift-giver is thinking: Look, if ceramic coffee mugs and socks and variable speed reversible drills aren't appropriate Father's Day gifts, what in God's name is?

Use your imagination. We fathers would simply feel better if we received something other than, oh, a yellow tie decorated with tiny blue sailboats.

Or a comb.

Please. We're asking nicely.

X-mas visit to mall of living dead

Journal of a Christmas shopping trip:

11:30 a.m. — Arrive at mall. Chaos. Parking lot looks like something from "The Road Warrior." All that's missing are the smoldering Humvees and a few corpses dumped on the side of the road. Thuggish woman in a Ford Taurus cuts me off and zips into handicapped parking space. She leaps out and practically sprints to the entrance.

Way to go, sweetie. Why should the people in wheelchairs hog all the good parking spots, right? Peace on Earth, good will toward men...

11:40 — All I can say is, what recession? They're even three deep in the Hickory Farms Store. *There's* something I could never understand. Who gives cheese and salami as a Christmas gift? ("Honey, couldn't find that pearl necklace, but here's a few sticks of pepperoni...")

Noon — Good God, we're all doomed! Santa has just arrived at his first-floor "Workshop." Some 200 kids, jacked up on cola and chocolate, surge forward, screaming: "SAN-TA! SAN-TA!" Put flaming torches in their hands, and they could double as a mob of Balkan villagers hunting down the Wolfman.

Santa's face drains of color. He manages a weak "Ho, ho, ho!" but his eyes are busy scanning the exits. Last day on the job? You bet. This time next week, he'll be working the deep fryer at Sizzlers.

12:15 p.m. — Sullen bimbo-in-training at Gap says black T-shirt I just bought is "out" now.

"Well, I need it for night work," I say. "See, I'm a cat burglar."

"Anyway," she says, "that'll be $11.03."

I ask if there's any place around to buy a ski mask.

"Try Penney's," she says.

12:30 — Lunch. The food court is packed. After grabbing a burger, I shoehorn myself into a table next to an ominous-looking man in camouflage jacket and cowboy hat.

Mentally, I rehearse emergency procedures for when Tex flips out and starts raking place with small-arms fire: Dive under table, scream "Don't shoot!" in both English and Spanish, assure Tex that I've been receiving the very same high-frequency messages through *my* tooth fillings.

1:00 — I'm in the lingerie department at Macy's. Feeling extreme discomfort. The sales people look at me like I'm wearing a rumpled raincoat and nothing on underneath, with a river of drool running down my chin. I want to run up to the dour-faced woman at the register and blurt out: "Look, this isn't for *me*! I'm not *like* that!"

Finally, as panic sets in, I pick up a racy little teddy that looks like it belongs on a Miss Penzoil calendar. My wife wouldn't wear this thing if the whole East Coast suffered a power blackout. But, hey, it's the thought that counts.

1:20 — Strictly for laughs, I stop back to see how Santa's doing. The answer: not so well. Santa seems extremely agitated. Noise level resembles a Saturn 5 rocket at liftoff. Hyperactive 3-year-old on Santa's lap pulls his nose and whines: "I *want* a Barney coloring book..."

Hoo, boy. Another ten minutes tops before Santa loses it and pulls out a straight razor.

1:40 — In the record and tape store now. Skulking through the aisles is the usual Night-of-the-Living-Dead crowd: disaffected punkers with green hair and nose rings; gangster wannabes dripping with gold; vacant-eyed heavy metal freaks; beered-up high school dropouts, etc.

If somebody opened a rehab clinic next door, they'd make a killing.

2:05 — I buy overpriced sweater from scowling salesman who apparently feels he should be CEO of Time-Warner and can't believe he's fallen so far as to actually be working in a men's store.

I ask if he has a box for the sweater. He says no, might have some in next Saturday. As gently as possible, I point out that next Saturday is day after Christmas, at which time the box will do me absolutely no good unless I punch holes in it and use it to house a turtle.

2:15 — Kids are like dogs: They can smell fear in a man. I'm in a toy store and three of the little monsters, having backed me into a corner, close in with plastic "Terminator"-style rocket launchers. It's like looking at three budding John Hinckleys. I grab a toy off the shelf and bully my way to the register.

2:30 — Nerves shot, hands trembling badly now. It's time to go. Scene in the parking lot is even more chaotic now. Car engines revving, brakes screeching, stereos thumping, people cursing, all under a swollen purple sky.

All we need are a few helicopter gunships dropping napalm and the Doors intoning: "This is the end..."

It may not be the end, but it's damn close.

A special time of year on TV

A look at the coming holiday specials on TV — check your local listings for air dates:

• "A Peanuts Christmas" (CBS). (Animated) Charlie Brown and the gang befriend a homeless man on Christmas Eve who soon finds them as irritating as everyone else does. Snoopy urinates on the man's only pair of shoes.

• "Billy Ray Cyrus' Country Christmas" (TNN). Billy Ray sweats to "Jingle Bells," "Santa Claus is Coming to Town" and his newest hit single, "More Achy Breaky Heart" before narrating a tractor pull at the Memphis Coliseum.

• "Mike Tyson's KO Christmas Special!" (ABC) Taped at the Indiana prison where he's serving a rape sentence, the former heavyweight boxing champ reads his holiday poems ("Pain: I Like to Give It," "Hellhole," "Ain't Nobody's Girlfriend") and shows off his papier maché Christmas decorations made in the prison art class. Guests: Spike Lee, Indiana Youth Center Chorus. Special appearance by Don King.

• "Frosty the Snowman" (CBS). (Animated) An unexpected heat wave has Frosty concerned about his health when his carrot nose melts off and both button eyes wash away. Frosty's voice: Charlton Heston.

• "The Andy Williams Christmas Special" (PBS). Taped at the Moon River Theatre in Branson, Mo., the venerable, low-key entertainer meanders through his traditional relaxed performance until everyone in the audience is sound asleep.

• "The Bob Hope Holiday Special" (NBC). Ninety years young, Bob delivers his traditional holiday package of cornball jokes, lame skits, second-rate cabaret singers, and giggling, busty young actresses. This unedited version has Bob bounding on stage and yelling: "How ya doin', Da Nang?" apparently thinking he's back in Vietnam during the Tet Offensive.

• "A Malibu Christmas with Susan Anton" (CBS). The has-been actress takes time out from her new job as Amway products sales rep to host an evening of singing and dancing. Homes caught in the recent brush fires smolder gaily in the background. Guests: Shari Lewis, Huey Lewis and the News, Louis Farrakhan.

• "How The Grinch Stole Christmas" (TBS). (Animated) The mean, green, half-ape half-cat returns to terrify the residents of Whoville, who suspect he's the byproduct of an accident at a nearby nuclear reactor. Voice of the Grinch: Secretary of Defense Les Aspin.

• "An Alabama Country Christmas" (TNN). Hairy country band Alabama fetes the holidays with some down-home singin' and hosts a whittlin' and hog-callin' contest. Guests: Vince Gill, stock car legend Richard Petty.

• "Def Comedy Christmas Jam" (HBO). The holidays come to the 'hood as Martin Lawrence hosts an evening of stand-up featuring foul-mouthed comics ruminating on such festive themes as Santa visiting a crackhouse, Santa getting wounded in a drive-by shooting, and Santa consorting with promiscuous women.

• "A Wayne's World Christmas" (MTV). The goofy cable-access legends from Aurora, Ill., kick out the jams in Wayne's basement rec room in a holiday tribute to Led Zeppelin, Jimi Hendrix, Aerosmith and Sharon Stone. The boys toast the Christmas season by sniffing cleaning fluid from a plastic bag, and Wayne's haunting electric guitar improvisation of "Silent Night" reduces Garth to tears.

• "A Mickey Mouse Christmas Carol" (The Disney Channel). (Animated) Dickens rolls over in his grave in this Disney remake of the classic tale, with Donald in the title role as skinflint Scrooge McDuck and Mickey cast as the downtrodden Bob Cratchit. One serious flaw: Donald's annoying nephews Huey, Dewey and Louie are improbably cast as McDuck's business partners.

• "Chevy Chase's Salute to Christmas" (Fox). Fresh from his disastrous experiment as a talk show host, Chevy hosts an evening of unfunny sight gags, off-key caroling, strained conversation, and forced merriment with guests Goldie Hawn, Whoopi Goldberg and Martin Mull. An impromptu 20-second crying jag during the intro, as well as his pointed death threat against Fox chairwoman Lucie Salhany, hint at Chevy's lingering bitterness over his show's cancellation.

• "Christmas Eve With Tony Danza" (NBC). In his thick Brooklyn accent, the former "Who's the Boss?" star reads "'Twas the Night Before Christmas" to puzzled orphans ("...an' all tru da house, not a creecher was stirrin', not even a freakin' *mouse*, ya see what I'm sayin'?") before inexplicably donning boxing gloves and sparring three rounds with Walter Matthau. Special appearance by the Fight Doctor, Ferdie Pacheco.

x

Holiday music goes to the dogs

In a chilling reminder that pain and suffering can originate anywhere, I turned on the car radio the other day and found myself listening to the Singing Dogs' rendition of "Jingle Bells."

This, of course, remains the single most horrible Christmas song of all time, as well as audible proof that there are certain things animals should never be asked to do.

For those fortunate enough to be unfamiliar with the "lyrics," imagine three or four skittish Labrador retrievers trapped in a burning building.

The dogs are barking frantically. Suddenly, the barking takes on a hauntingly familiar cadence, which corresponds roughly to... well, *you* be the judge:

"Wroof, wroof, wroof,

"Wroof, wroof, wroof,

"Wroof, WROOF, wroof, wroof, wroof."

As you can imagine, the effect of all this on the central nervous system is incredible.

Instantly, I could feel a familiar pounding in my head and the first wave of nausea washing over me.

By the second chorus, it was all I could do not to stomp on the gas and send the car slamming into the nearest bridge abutment.

A strong candidate for second-worst Christmas song of all time is the supremely annoying "Grandma Got Run Over By A Reindeer."

This is the thoroughly unconvincing tale of a reindeer that supposedly runs amok on Christmas Eve and tramples an elderly woman.

Incredibly, the singers themselves (Patsy and Elmo were the original, ahem, *artists*) make light of the entire tragedy.

The song is so irritating that the listener actively roots for the reindeer to make a clean sweep of things by goring both the narrators and their grandpa — and leaving the corpses out where the buzzards can find them.

Between its bleak lyrics ("You can say there's no such thing as Santa...") and uninspired melody, the song quickly leaves the listener fumbling through the medicine cabinet for any available anti-depressants.

While we're on the theme of animals, a particularly insipid version of "Jingle Bells" by Alvin and the Chipmunks is still heard on occasion during the holiday season, with stunning disregard for the ill will it generates toward the semi-terrestrial, squirrel-like rodents.

The song is sung (if that's the word) in such a screechy, unpleasant voice that it invariably leaves even the most devoted animal rights activist ready to pick up a shotgun and blast it down the nearest chipmunk hole.

Turning to more traditional bad Christmas music, "The Little Drummer Boy," as sung by Perry Como, has its moments — well, *seconds* actually.

But by the 12th or so "a-rum-pah-pum-pum," one begins to entertain dark fantasies of stealing into Mr. Como's bedroom, picking up a pillow and smothering the man as he sleeps.

Until now, I have refrained from mentioning the incredibly gooey "I saw Mommy Kissing Santa Claus," for fear of having the reader put down this newspaper, run into the kitchen, and do serious harm to himself or herself with a butcher knife.

The sappy version sung by the dysfunctional Jackson Five some years ago is the worst of the worst.

This, of course, was before Michael Jackson cut out the picture of a young Diana Ross, burst into the offices of a startled Beverly Hills cosmetic surgeon and shouted: "Here! Make me look like her!"

Whipped along by the hormonal stirrings of the young Jacksons, the song vaguely alludes to some sort of tryst between a woman and a man dressed in a Santa outfit, who may or may not be the woman's lawfully-wedded husband.

In any event, the Jacksons' cat-caught-in-the-screen-door falsettos and syrupy improvisations ("I *did*! I *did*! I *did* see Mommy kissing Santa Claus!") represent the closest thing to a near-death experience one can imagine — although without the ensuing sense of well-being reported by most victims of serious illnesses and car wrecks.

Of course, we could go on and on listing bad Christmas music:

• Jim Nabors droning through "Silver Bells," which has surely been incorporated into a training film about the dangers of narcolepsy.

• Barry Manilow's halting rendition of "Silent Night," which suggests a man fighting through the haze of a barbiturate overdose.

• The bizarre duo of Frank Sinatra-Cyndi Lauper singing "Santa Claus Is Coming to Town," lending instant credence to the rumor that the Chairman of the Board may indeed have suffered a breakdown recently.

And they wonder why the music industry is in such a slump.

With the new Santa, you better watch out

It was the night before Christmas and inside Santa Claus' workshop at the North Pole, the elves were grumbling bitterly.

Lorenzo, the shop steward, said: "The man refuses to take us seriously. Time and again we've asked him for a 401(k) retirement plan, night differential for all shifts after 4 p.m., and a modern conveyor belt that would facilitate transport of the toys from the shop to the sleigh."

"Plus, we want the place tested for radon," added Roy, shivering slightly. Smoking was now prohibited in all 16 buildings at Santa Enterprises Inc., and Roy had just returned from grabbing a few puffs outside, where it was 60 below zero.

In the room next door, Santa listened to the griping as he went through a brisk, 40-minute workout on the Nautilus.

He permitted himself a quick look in the floor-length mirror. Gone was the fat, red-faced Santa of a few years ago. The new Santa was a trim, hard 165 pounds. The beard had been replaced by a neat goatee. His hair was heavily moussed and combed back in the style of Knicks coach Pat Riley.

"Slick," that's what the elves called him now. It didn't help that there was a new Mrs. Claus around — the *fourth* Mrs. Claus, a real looker named Kelly who worked at the Hair Cuttery.

After knocking off 50 sit-ups, Santa decided to confront the elves. Lorenzo was holding up a copy of the Federal Wage and Hour Laws.

"Y'know, I *do* and *do* and *do* for you people, and this is the thanks I get," Santa said. "I could sub-contract this work to Taiwan or Guatemala. But I keep you bums on because, well, because that's the kind of guy I am. Look, if you feel you have legitimate grievances, put 'em in writing. Right now, I have toys to deliver."

Santa grabbed his beeper, and went outside, where a light snow was falling. Donner, with the other reindeer, approached him as he neared the stables. It seemed the reindeer were circulating a petition demanding that Santa lighten the sleigh.

"For the sake of argument, say we're lugging 3,500 My Size Barbies," Donner said. "At roughly six pounds each, you're talking... six fives are 30, carry the three... 21,000 pounds right there.

"And that's not counting your Talking Barneys, your Tonka trucks, and so on."

Santa swore softly. He told Donner to get over to the sleigh, as it was time to shove off. But the reindeer were grumbling louder now, and suddenly a voice shouted: "We ain't goin' anywhere, Slick!"

In an instant, Santa pulled a pistol from his waistband and fired three shots in the air. The reindeer froze. Lorenzo, taking in the scene from a workshop window, wrote in his journal: "Pathetic. The man is out of control."

"Now listen up!" Santa barked. "The first reindeer that gives me a hard time, I'll drill 'im right between the eyes, so help me! Our job is to deliver toys to the good little boys and girls all over the world!"

Santa had a temper, there was no doubt about that. One foggy Christmas Eve, he had actually whacked Rudolph with a tree branch when Rudolph yelped: "I'm not going out in this — you're out of your mind!"

So the reindeer moved quickly to the sleigh, as they had no desire to taste hot lead. The takeoff went smoothly, although they came close to shearing off the satellite dish on Santa's roof.

The skies were crowded that night. At one point, the sleigh came within 25 yards of an Air Canada flight; they could see little kids making faces at them in the rear window seats. Then, coming into Miami, they nearly hit a Cessna trailing a lighted banner over the beach that said: "Happy Hour at Pirate's Cove, 2-for-1 drinks! Sat nite wet T-shirt contest!"

Their only break of the night came when they put down in a 7-Eleven parking lot and Santa grabbed a yogurt and decaf coffee.

There were the usual incidents, of course. In Stockholm, Santa slipped down the chimney and this big, crazy Swede came at him with a fireplace poker. In Buenos Aires, they tripped a burglar alarm and had to skedaddle. In Ireland, IRA sympathizers mistook the sleigh for a British helicopter and began firing.

Well after dawn, Santa and the reindeer arrived back at the North Pole, bone-tired.

Lorenzo met him at the door, waving a fresh list of demands that included the purchase of new lathes, a complete renovation of the warehouse, and five weeks paid vacation for each senior elf.

Just then Kelly came in and handed Santa a Coors Light.

"Honey, one of my customers at the Cuttery teaches elementary school," she said. "They're having a Career Day program. Maybe you could talk to the kids about what you do with the, um, toys and stuff — what is it again?"

Kelly was very sweet, Santa decided. But you'd never mistake her for the editor of the *Harvard Law Review*.

Get Your
Motor Runnin'

Life in the slow lane not too swift

The last time I got a speeding ticket, I had come sailing over a bridge and through a radar trap on the interstate when a state trooper motioned me to pull over.

"What's the problem, officer?" I said.

He gave me the kind of look you'd give a roach walking across your salad.

Then in a disgusted voice, he said: "67 in a 55." The way you'd say: "There's a headless corpse sticking out of your trunk."

It was at this point in the proceedings that I made my big mistake.

The baby was wailing in the back seat and the other two kids were throwing bolo punches at each other, and I guess I just kind of lost it. Because I said: "Hey, I was just keeping up with traffic."

Well. The trooper didn't like that one bit. His face went beet-red and his breathing suddenly came in shallow, angry bursts — *yi! yi!yi!* — like a Pekingese with a head cold.

"The... speed... limit... is... 55," he said with barely controlled fury.

Then he ripped the ticket from his book, handed it to me, and stomped back to his car.

So my advice is, if you get pulled over for speeding, don't ever tell the cop you were just keeping up with traffic. They don't seem to go for that one at all.

The fact is, though, that anyone who actually does 55 on an interstate highway these days is taking his life in his hands.

As a little experiment, I decided to drive precisely at the speed limit on I-95 between Baltimore and Delaware, one of the nation's busiest stretches of highway.

I also kept a tape-recorded journal of the entire terrifying ride:

9:30 a.m. — Here we go. My palms are sweating and I'm feeling nauseous. But you know? It's a *good* kind of nauseous. As we merge into the far right-hand lane and accelerate to 55, I brace myself for the inevitable squeal of brakes locking up behind me.

9:34 — Well, that didn't take long. A white Chevy Citation has just roared up and is now sitting 18 inches from my rear bumper. The driver, swarthy and goateed, looks like he's just returned from the "America's Most Wanted" studios. Finally, he passes and shoots me the requisite dirty look. "Hey, pal," I say, "speed limit's 55."

Why do I feel like the fourth-grader who shoots his hand in the air after the final bell and says: "Mrs. Fanutti, aren't you going to give us homework?"

9:41 — This is it: My first brush with a wild-eyed, amphetamine-crazed trucker. An 18-wheeler has just roared up, the driver down-shifting furiously to avoid slamming into me and igniting a fiery inferno visible in Vermont. He sits on my tail for a minute, then bangs the gears furiously and passes me. Is this what they mean by a near-death experience?

9:53 — You know what cracks me up? Those warning signs that say: "Speed monitored by aircraft." Have you ever once seen a police Cessna overhead with a cop yelling into a bullhorn: "You in the brown Toyota — PULL OVER!"?

I don't *think* so. Not that a solid citizen like myself has anything to worry about.

10:10 — Uh oh, a state trooper is behind me now. You talk about acting suspicious — he probably thinks I'm just back from Miami with 10 kilos of cocaine and a crate of assault rifles. Who else does 55 these days but drug dealers and gun runners? OK, my wife, but that's about it.

I'm nervous, although God knows why. If the cop pulls me over and searches the car, all he'll find is $40 worth of Fisher-Price toys. Go ahead, flat-foot. Hit the lights. Make my day.

10:33 — Tell me something: Did they change the motor vehicle statutes? Is the right lane *only* for mass murderers now? A Ted Bundy look-alike in a black Camaro is tailgating me now. Probably jotting down my license plate number so he can track me down next time he warms up the chain saw.

10:50 — Just crossed the border into Delaware. The warning signs here say: "Speeders will be executed and buried in shallow graves." Hoo, boy. The folks up here might be taking this whole highway safety thing a *lit-tle* too seriously. Might be time to think about decaf in the morning, too.

10:53 — Another 18-wheeler just roared up. This guy's a little cranky; probably hasn't slept since the Carter administration. He keeps flashing his lights, and finally swerves around me at 70 mph, cutting off a mini-van loaded with priests. That's a one-way ticket to the eternal flames, buddy.

11:00 — That's it, I've had it. My nerves are shot. Every time somebody passes me, I'm ducking involuntarily to avoid gunshots. Time to step heavy on the gas pedal and join the rest of society.

It may not be legal, but it's a hell of a lot safer.

Hint to drivers: open your eyes

Tell me if this sounds reasonable. If it doesn't, fine, I won't bring it up again: If you're driving along and a squirrel darts in front of your car, it's probably not a good idea to let go of the steering wheel, cover your eyes and scream.

This is what my wife — a very bright woman, but... well, never mind — did the other day on a busy stretch of road.

As the lone passenger in the car, I became somewhat alarmed at the realization that a screaming blind woman who refused to hold the steering wheel was now in charge of my life. Then I began screaming myself, as I had this vision of the car leaving the road, becoming airborne and plowing through the picture window of someone's living room.

Thankfully, we did not die and neither did the squirrel, although when it was all over I wanted to kill the damn thing myself and parade his sorry little carcass around on the end of a broomstick.

As for my wife, she couldn't understand why anyone would get upset that she let go of the wheel, covered her eyes and screamed when the squirrel appeared.

"It's a perfectly normal reaction," she said.

"That is the reaction of a lunatic," I said, and of course we have not spoken since. Let me give you my reading on the whole thing, and see if it squares with yours.

It seems to me that when the driver of a car lets go of the steering wheel, he or she creates what might be called, in technical terms, a "safety hazard."

This is because the car will then go pretty much wherever it wants to, and if the car plows into a telephone pole or smashes into a ditch, the driver certainly can't shake his or her head in amazement and think: "How about *that?*"

Now... the covering of the eyes.

Maybe it's me, but I have a real problem with people who cover their eyes while operating a motor vehicle.

By covering your eyes, you reduce your field of vision from roughly 180 degrees (minus the rearview mirror) to, oh, zero degrees.

And a zero-degree field of vision seems unacceptable while driving, particularly when some suicidal squirrel runs in front of your car. Not to put too fine a point on it, but this is why you don't see a lot of motorists driving with blindfolds or, for that matter, with paper bags over their heads, either.

As for the panicky screaming, this, too, seemed an error in judgment.

Understand, screaming in and of itself is not necessarily bad, and there might even be a place for it in a car, such as if you're stalled on railroad tracks and you happen to look up and there's a train bearing down on you at 70 miles per hour.

But the fact is, I was already a little jittery when I saw her let go of the steering wheel and cover her eyes.

At that point, I thought only of death, and not the squirrel's death, either. I didn't give a rat's behind about the squirrel.

Add a piercing scream to all this and it jacks up the anxiety levels considerably.

Now, don't get me wrong here. No one wants to see a squirrel flattened by a car. What kind of animal do you take me for, anyway?

But by the same token, I'd prefer that we not lose control of the car and plunge over a cliff and tumble end-over-end down a steep ravine before igniting in a huge fireball visible for many miles.

If we have to take out some dopey squirrel in order to avoid this, my feeling is: By all means, take out the squirrel.

There are, after all, hundreds of thousands of squirrels, maybe even millions of them. Losing one squirrel is no big deal.

Granted, it's a big deal for that particular squirrel, who, in the last fleeting seconds of his life, sees a pair of muddy Goodyear radials heading at him.

But there are so many *other* squirrels. And let's face it, they all look the same, with their curly tails and their nuts in the cheeks and the whole business.

This is not intended as some vicious polemic on squirrels. The point is... well, I forget the point right now. Frankly, I'm still a little unnerved by the whole incident and you would be too, unless you're some kind of robot or something.

Driven crazy by car phones

I was driving along the Beltway in my usual cautious manner — eyes alertly scanning for traffic hazards, hands at the 10 and 2 o'clock positions on the steering wheel — when this black BMW up ahead began drifting between lanes.

As it was nine in the morning, I assumed the driver was not drunk or jabbing a syringe in one arm, although in this day and age that might be a charitable assumption.

Instead, I figured this driver was talking on a car phone, which has become the new death rattle of the '90s.

When car phones became popular, my thinking was: Great. This is just what we need — another diversion for motorists as they careen down the highway at 70 mph.

Apparently it wasn't enough to have them reading stupid bumper stickers that said "Don't Laugh — It's Paid For," or staring at terrified Garfields plastered against rear windshields.

Now we were giving them car phones, ensuring that their concentration will wander even further and that highways will become even more littered with twisted hulks of charred metal.

In fact, with the advent of car phones, my first instinct was to compile a list of companies that manufactured body bags so that I could invest heavily in their stock and become a wealthy man.

Now I keep waiting for the day when auto manufacturers install TV sets in the dashboards so that drivers, while keeping an occasional eye on the road, can also keep up with Geraldo's latest freak show or what's happening on "Murphy Brown."

The next logical step would be Nintendo units located directly adjacent to the steering wheel, allowing truly ambitious drivers to gun down intergalactic space invaders while weaving between roaring 18-wheelers on the interstate.

God help us if that happens. Talk about carnage. They might as well just build the cemeteries directly alongside the highway. Certainly this would cut down on funeral expenses, as emergency crews could simply crowbar you out of the wreck and plant you a few feet away under a tasteful headstone like: "Here lies Harry 'Joystick' McCoy. He was playing 'Super Mario Brothers.'"

Anyway, as I was saying, I watched this black BMW drift between lanes for about two miles when a voice in my head cried: "Enough! Let's investigate the cause of this nonsense."

So I stomped on the accelerator. This did very little at first, because I drive an old Toyota with a four-cylinder engine that produces about the same horsepower as a child's Big Wheel.

But finally I caught up to the Beemer. Sure enough, behind the wheel was some jerk talking on a car phone.

Taking pains to stay well out of his way, I observed an amazing phenomenon. As other drivers swerved to avoid him, they would shoot him dirty looks.

But the man did not notice the dirty looks. Because he was paying absolutely no attention to what was going on around him.

Instead, he was engaged in a spirited conversation that included a lot of angry shouting and hand-waving and fists crashing against the dashboard.

Mercifully, the BMW got off at the next exit, apparently managing not to slam into the bridge abutment, judging by the lack of a fresh obituary in the newspaper.

Now, I understand that car phones are here to stay. The toothpaste is out of the tube, so to speak. This is not another tired harangue on that score.

Let me just ask a few simple favors of you car phone users:

No. 1: I would appreciate if you'd occasionally glance up at the road, particularly when you see a brown 1980 Toyota Corolla with a prominent dent in the right quarter panel and a very tired-looking man behind the wheel.

No. 2: If the conversation is getting fairly heated, perhaps you could hang up for a while and resume the discussion later from the comfort of your own driveway, where you would not be a threat to plow into the rear of my car and ignite a towering inferno visible in several states.

No. 3: If we happen to be driving near each other during a driving rainstorm or blizzard, perhaps, until traffic conditions improve, you could hold off calling your wife to see what's for dinner.

Besides, it's probably leftovers.

Cable-ready on the highway

A few days ago, in the midst of a rare episode of clear thinking, I went and bought a set of jumper cables.

No one ever actually *buys* jumper cables, of course.

Instead, what people do is wait for that awful day when their car battery (for whatever reason) dies in some nearly deserted mall parking lot.

Then they stand there in the fading light and frantically flag down a total stranger, who looks vaguely like the police sketch of a suspected slasher in that morning's paper.

Mercifully, though, the stranger stops and pulls a set of well-worn jumper cables from his trunk instead of the serrated 10-inch commando knife they were certain he'd brandish.

And after he cheerfully jump starts their car and leaves, they think: "Gee, I should really get my *own* jumper cables..."

This was the sort of convoluted, "did-a-safe drop on-his-head?" thinking I displayed for many years.

Then, the other day I burst into the auto department at Sears and cornered the startled sales clerk near the SteadyRider shock-absorber display.

Stabbing a stubby finger at page 1349 of the store catalog, I shouted: "Gimme those babies right there, chief!"

Unfortunately, the man was recently arrived from the Indian subcontinent and mistook my enthusiasm for some sort of strong-arm move on his watch and gold bracelet.

This is what can happen in the tense environment of a department store when people of different cultures meet, and one of them happens to be frothing at the mouth from excitement.

Anyway, we finally straightened out the misunderstanding and Rishi (that was the man's name) was then kind enough to show me the jumper cables.

They're real beauties, too: Heavy-duty six-gauge cables. Sixteen feet long. Copper-plated steel saws. I'm telling you, these babies could jump start a Saturn 5 rocket.

At the very least, the new cables will help me avoid disturbing incidents like the one that took place the last time my car battery died.

This occurred in the parking lot of a rest area on the New Jersey Turnpike — the Richard Stockton rest area, I think. Or maybe it was the Molly Pitcher rest area. Look, all I know is ,it was one of those pit stops inexplicably named after a Revolutionary War hero, even though the most historic thing in the joint is a Bob's Big Boy.

As it was eleven o'clock at night and there was only one other car around — a late-model Cadillac driven by what appeared to be two Gambino Family soldiers — my first thought was: I'm a dead man.

So I popped the hood and stood there staring at the engine for many minutes, as if in my growing panic I could actually *will* the battery back to life.

Suddenly, out of nowhere, a big, white customized minivan lurched to a stop next to me.

Naturally, my first reaction — remember, this was *New Jersey* — was to dive to the pavement, do a quick shoulder roll under my car, and shout: "Don't shoot! *No dispares tu pistola! Allez-vous-en!*"

It was while struggling with the Mandarin Chinese translation of "Please don't kill me!" that I realized no actual guns had been fired.

Instead, a beefy guy with 27 gold chains around his neck leaned out the window of the minivan and said: "Whassa matta, pal? Needa jump?"

Well, it was all I could do not to drop to my knees and begin buffing his shoes right there.

The good Samaritan turned out to be a gregarious fellow we'll call Dominic, who lived in Bay Shore, Long Island.

Unfortunately for me, Dominic and his family were just returning from a 10-day vacation in Florida, and now seemed relentlessly determined to fill me in on every detail of the trip.

So, as Dominic fished a greasy set of jumper cables from his minivan, I heard all about their adventures in Disney World ("da lines, fuh-ged-a-bou-dit!") and Sea World ("nuttin' but fish, fish, fish").

Then, as we connected the clamps to the battery terminals, I heard about their stops at Aunt Bee's Gingerbread House ("graydiss gin-cha-bread in da world"), Walt's Famous World of Reptiles ("biggess snake I evuh sawr!") and South of the Border ("a freakin' rip-off, right Angie?").

I don't know... at some point in the conversation I must have drifted into hyper-sleep.

The next thing I remember is my car engine roaring to life and Dominic slapping me on the shoulder and shouting: "Ya oughta gitcher own jumpah cables, pal!"

Absolutely.

I've become a "man in a van"

There comes a sobering moment in every man's existence when he realizes that he's already seen the best life has to offer, and that everything from there on is a long, dark slide into the cold ground.

That time has arrived for me. I'm buying a minivan.

Plymouth Voyager, Toyota Previa, Dodge Caravan... what difference does it make? My life is over.

Four-speed overdrive transmission, 3.0-liter V6 engine, wood-grain side panels, extended luggage rack... so what?

What did the author William Styron call the gloom that came to envelop him? A veil of darkness descending slowly? Yes, I can see how that would fit. There is an ineffable sadness associated with the sight of a man in a minivan.

When a man sits behind the wheel of a minivan, all pretense of being even *vaguely* hip vanishes.

Somehow, even before he sings out to the children: "Everybody have their seat belts on?" he loses his identity. He loses his soul. He loses his swagger and his sense of cool.

He becomes a... *dad*, the doppelganger of Homer Simpson and Cliff Huxtable and Dagwood Bumstead and a million other nameless, faceless wretches who (it would seem) exist solely to fire up the grill on weekends.

Teen-age thugs snicker as he drives by, greatly amused by the minivan's bumper stickers proclaiming recent family visits to Aunt Bee's Gingerbread House or Walt's Famous World of Reptiles.

Single people stare in horror as he pulls up to the Dairy Queen, and the minivan disgorges five brawling children (three of his own, two of the neighbors') for a tranquilizing round of chocolate shakes.

Women no longer glance over and smile as he pulls up to a traffic light. In fact, as far as *young* women are concerned, there might as well be a sign on the side of the minivan that says "St. Joseph's Seminary."

A man driving a van becomes, for all intents and purposes, invisible.

Eagle Summit, GMC Safari, Mazda MPV... is this what it's all about?

Optional moon-roof, rear wheel anti-lock brakes, swing-out and fold-down Dutch door... I guess it *should* matter. But it doesn't.

Sometimes, if I *really* want to feel low, I think back on the evolution of the cars I've owned.

There was high school and the Age of Aquarius and a succession of beat-up old Volkswagen Beetles with amateurish psychedelic paint jobs.

During college and tuition struggles, there was an economical Ford Pinto — the Death Machine. A young man prayed that a soft tap from behind by a careless motorist wouldn't produce a towering fireball visible throughout the county. Or, if it *did, that* it would be all over before his 9 a.m. Introduction to Chaucer class.

Then a few years later, it happened. I bought a brand new Camaro. Metallic gold paint job. Black interior. Powerful V8 engine. Four on the floor. Hurst shifter. Zero to 60 in what... six seconds?

It was the greatest car a guy could own — until I drove it into a stone wall. How? Don't ask. It's too painful.

The repair job cost $2,100. The garage should have sent a priest along with the bill, because the car was never the same. Six months later, it was sold to an earnest young man who announced he needed it to attend culinary school.

It didn't strike me as the kind of car a chef would necessarily favor, but the world was changing fast.

After then there was a sporty Nissan 200-SX, a wonderful car for a newly married man, except that it had all the leg room of the Apollo 12.

The newly married man and his wife then had a child, and then another child. It was time to buy a Subaru station wagon. A *station wagon*, for God's sake!

The station wagon should have sent up a flare that things were changing dramatically, that there was to be a great dimming in the joy of driving. Then a third child came along and suddenly it was an effort to shoehorn everyone into the station wagon.

Now it's a minivan.

Mitsubishi Expo LRV, Pontiac Trans Sport, Oldsmobile Silhoutte... it's so hard to get out of bed in the morning.

Integrated child-seat option, heavy-duty upgraded upholstery, rear climate-control system... Gertrude Stein was right. There is no *there* there.

I go around to the various dealerships now. I test-drive the minivans. I gaze listlessly at the brochures they hand me.

"Go ahead, take 'er out for a spin!" the salesman says cheerfully, tossing me the keys to yet another hulking seven-seater with all the sex appeal of a bakery truck.

What's the point? I think.

What was it that Nietzsche said: "A great-souled hero must transcend the slavish thinking of those around him?"

Yeah, sure. I wonder what *he* was driving.

Reluctantly selling the perfect car

I am currently trying to sell my car, a process that involves the usual amount of lying and deception.

Fortunately, I have no problem with lying and deception; in fact, the two have always been second nature to me, like breathing and eating.

There are days when I actually spend vast stretches of time, six and seven hours, without speaking the truth even once. And as far as swindling goes, well, everyone is fair game, including nuns and small children.

So I feel good about the chances of selling this car — particularly if the buyer is not very bright or vulnerable in some other way. Visually impaired, for example.

You didn't ask, but the reason the car is for sale has nothing to do with how it's running, which, believe me, is like a top.

No, what happened is this: Despite making the kind of salary that compares favorably only to the proprietor of a child's lemonade stand, I went out and bought a new car.

This was totally unplanned. One minute I was driving by this car dealership, the next minute a small cloud descended around my head and I was signing a piece of paper while a half-dozen salesmen in loud sport coats elbowed each other and snickered in the background.

The new car plunged me even deeper into debt than usual.

Naturally, my first thought was: *somebody* around here needs to get a second job. So I looked in the newspaper and found a job on a loading dock that would be absolutely perfect for my wife.

You couldn't beat the hours — midnight to four in the morning. Plus you didn't have to lift anything heavier than refrigerators and file cabinets, that sort of thing.

As I said, it sounded perfect for her. But every time I brought up the subject, we got into an argument. So I give up. Don't ask me how we'll make the payments on this new car.

Anyway, now I have to unload the, um, quality automobile I drove previously.

My first step was to place an ad in the classified section of the local rag.

Almost every single car ad in there said something like: "1990 Camaro. Excellent condition. Low mileage. Loaded. Greatest car ever built."

So to make my ad stand out, I had them write: "1980 Toyota Corolla. Formerly owned by Pope John Paul II. $600."

Legally, I was probably on shaky ground here. But you worry about things like that when the time comes.

The problem with selling your car through a newspaper ad is that you have strangers — some of them clearly disturbed — showing up at your house at all hours.

I came out of the house the other morning when suddenly this figure lunged at me from near the garbage cans.

My first instinct — as it is whenever I'm confronted by members of the general public — was to do a quick shoulder roll onto the lawn in case he popped off a few shots.

Then I ran down the street screaming: "SOMEBODY CALL THE POLICE!"

But this guy kept running after me. And he was fast, very fast, maybe even a former track star, and he was yelling: "BOTSCAR! BOTSCAR!"

It was fairly obvious that I'd been marked for death by some lunatic cult whose assassins used daggers and the signature cry of "BOTSCAR!"

Finally, after a couple of blocks, it dawned on me that he was screaming: "I'M HERE ABOUT THE CAR!"

I was going to have him arrested for scaring me half to death. But when the cops came, they said you couldn't arrest someone for being a jerk and shouting gibberish. And you wonder why the country is going to hell in a handbasket.

Anyway, in addition to cult members, we've had several other unannounced visitors, all the type of people you'd want to run through a metal detector before letting into your home.

The other problem with selling a car is that potential buyers expect you to be knowledgeable about it.

This one ol' boy was checking out the car the other day, and I knew I was in trouble from the get-go.

Not only was he wearing bib overalls and a John Deere hat, but he was one of these people who *insists* on seeing the engine first — like I might have taken it out and hidden it in the basement or something devious.

Anyway, he popped the hood and poked around for a couple of minutes. Suddenly, he sent a stream of tobacco juice flying (which caught my shoe, thank you very much) and asked: "She burn a lot of oil?"

"Geez, you got me, Tex," I said. "There's no black tornado following me around on the road, if that's what you mean."

Look, I can barely work the gas cap, never mind worry about how much oil I'm burning. All I know about cars is that you get in and drive them until they break down, after which you find something else to drive.

What I *do* know is that this is an excellent, excellent buy.

You have my word on that.

The Love Thing

Married life? Take it from me

What I try to stress to young people is that marriage is like... like a big empty canvas, OK? And it's up to the two of you to decide what you're gonna splash on it — the bright, vibrant hues of marital bliss, or the dark, brooding colors of an empty, meaningless co-existence.

Granted, it's a pretty heavy analogy, but that's what I was trying to get across to Tom at the bachelor party, only he was drinking shots of anisette with his beer while shooting pool, and his concentration seemed a tad erratic.

Plus "Runnin' on Empty" by Jackson Browne was playing on the jukebox, the volume was cranked up pretty loud, and you could hardly hear yourself think.

"You and Eileen are perfect together," I said.

"Arleen," he said.

"Right. Great. Catholic?"

"No, I'm Episcopalian."

"I mean Eileen."

"Arleen? Yeah, she's Catholic."

"Lemme tell you, Tom, marriage is like a..."

"Three ball in the side."

"...big empty canvas, OK?"

"A big, empty *what?*"

"Canvas. And it's up to the..."

"*Kansas?* A big, empty Kansas?"

"Look, forget that, OK? What I'm trying to say is that marriage is an awesome responsibility."

"Table leans to the left, you notice?"

"It's all about compromising, Tom."

"Uh-huh."

"Like, if you want to watch 'MacGyver,' only she wants to watch some movie with Farah Fawcett running around with a can of Sunoco 190, ready to burn her husband in bed. The two of you gotta compromise. Watch 'Coach' or something."

"'Coach.' That's a good show."

"Little things get on your nerves when you're married, though. You come home at three in the morning and right away she starts badgering you: 'Where were you? Where were you?'"

"I *hate* that stuff, man."

"You prob'ly have some questions about sex when you're married, huh?"

"Not really."

"Sex when you're married is like going to the 7-Eleven. Not as much variety, but at three in the morning, it's always there. Someone on TV once said that."

"I'm hitting the 7-Eleven right after this."

"Sex is a small part of marriage, anyway, Tom."

"Get me a burrito and a Big Gulp."

"A *very* small part, heh, heh."

"Maybe one of them Hostess fruit pies, too."

"Something about this conversation... I don't know."

"Nine ball up here."

"Like it's not very *focused* or something."

"They still got that Test Your Blood Pressure machine? At the 7-Eleven?"

"Marriage does funny things to people, Tom. For instance, my wife refuses to take out the garbage."

"This my beer?"

"Garbage can be piled to the ceiling — yeah, it's yours — she won't take it out. Says it's a *man's* job."

"Arleen wants me to get rid of my Bronco."

"Me, I see the garbage as gender-neutral."

"Says we gotta buy a 'family' car."

"Chicken bones, coffee grinds, orange peels, how does disposing of that suddenly become a man's... your *Bronco?!* All due respect, Tom, but I'd tell Eileen to shove it."

"Arleen."

"Man's Bronco is his own business!"

"Amen to that."

"Take away a man's Bronco, you take away his *soul*."

"You're preaching to the choir now, brother."

"Tom, we talk about sex in marriage yet?"

"Don't believe we did."

"That's 'cause there is none! Ha, ha... just a little married guy's humor there."

"Yo, they still have them chili dogs at the 7-Eleven?"

"Look, you don't need to hear an old guy like me babbling on and on. Here's to you and Eileen."

"Arleen."

"Lemme get this straight: It's *Arleen?*"

"Yeah, Arleen. That's her name."

"Huh! I coulda sworn it was..."

"Eight ball in the corner."

If memory serves, it was at this point that we all moved over to the bowling machine, which is when the conversation turned to the barmaid with the big chest.

I got home very late. The next day at softball practice, Tom said he appreciated our little talk, even though he only heard bits and pieces of it.

"Man, you were *deep*," he said.

You get as deep as you have to in those situations.

Our air is hot and tense

I'll tell you what Nancy and I can't talk about — and it has nothing to do with money or sex.

We can't talk about air conditioning. Oh, we can talk about anything else: religion, politics, even that little twerp Regis Philbin, who she thinks is the cat's meow.

Once, over a couple of bottles of wine, we even had a long discussion about Tom Selleck, the gist of it being that I thought the guy was way overrated, even a little homely if the light didn't catch him just so. She said I was drunk and went off to watch "Knots Landing." She has this unexplainable thing for Tom Selleck. Still, at least we got it out in the open.

But you can't talk about air conditioning in my house without someone getting all huffy and stomping out of the room. I don't know what the world is coming to when two adults can't discuss air conditioning, but that's the way it is.

The problem, in a nutshell, is this: When the weather gets hot, I like to turn on the air conditioning.

This is why central air conditioning was invented, for those days when the sun turns into a bright fireball in the sky and the humidity is thick enough to crawl into your pocket, and a normal human being needs a break from the oppression.

But apparently not everyone shares this enlightened viewpoint on air conditioning. Because as soon as I turn on the air and leave the room, my wife sprints to the thermostat. And turns off the air. And pretty soon the house is evincing all the steamy charm of a mango grove in El Salvador.

I come back in the room, reeling from the heat, and turn the air back on.

I leave the room, she turns it off.

It's a hell of a way to live, let me tell you. No one should have to live that way. Afraid to turn your back on your own thermostat. It's just not right.

As I said, though, you can't talk to her about air conditioning. Although Lord knows I've tried. I've tried talking about it until I'm blue in the face.

The air conditioning makes the house too cold, she says. If you're so hot, she says, open a window.

Meanwhile, it's 115 degrees outside. Dogs and cats are keeling over, cattle are dropping in their tracks, vultures are circling overhead. The sidewalks are littered with people who have passed out. Ambulances are screaming through the streets, babies are wailing, it's like a damn jungle out there with this heat.

And she wants me to open a window.

So I tell her, see, here's the problem with opening a window. It's 115 degrees outside. If I open a window, pretty soon it's going to feel like 115 degrees in *here*.

Instead of the sultry 97 degrees or whatever it is now.

But my wife, she doesn't want to hear about it. I turn on the air conditioning, she starts shivering for emphasis, as if we're on an ice floe somewhere.

You know what the real problem is? She's got the circulatory system of an iguana. That's the real problem. It's a medical aberration, is what I'm saying.

A normal human being begins to feel uncomfortable once the heat reaches 95 degrees or so. A normal human being would then turn on the air conditioning instead of sweating like a galley slave.

An iguana, on the other hand, enjoys severe heat and will actually bask in it atop the nearest mango leaf or wherever these creatures live.

"I'd go see a doctor if I had your circulation problem," I told my wife. "Not that I'm an alarmist. But you need some help."

Anyway, the other day the two of us sat down for another little chat about these thermostat wars.

"Look," I said, "this is ridiculous. How about arriving at a compromise? I'll turn the air conditioning on and you leave it alone. That way we'll get along just swell."

"Fine," she said. "No problem. I'm sick of fighting about it anyway."

I couldn't believe my ears. "You won't turn the air off anymore when it's 97 degrees in here and the flies are dropping off the ceiling?"

"No," she said. "You win. We'll try the air conditioning."

Well, sir, you can imagine how this made me feel. The long national nightmare was over! I had to check the urge to start turning cartwheels right then and there.

Instead, I cranked the air conditioning on full blast and left the house, a swagger to my walk and a song in my heart.

Which was a premature reaction, as it turned out. Because when I returned an hour later, the air conditioning was off. And the windows were wide open.

And the house had the same breezy feel as a rice paddy in Thailand.

I'm glad she finally caved in.

Alas, she's reading another man

I'm sorry if I seem a little down this holiday season, but I just found out my wife is cheating on me. She's reading another man.

I started stumbling across the tell-tale signs weeks ago: the stray bookmarks, the prescription reading glasses, the crumpled notices about overdue library books.

Soon she was coming home with smudged ink stains on her fingertips and that squinty look you get when you're reading under a 40-watt bulb instead of something that gives off less glare.

One day I came home a little earlier than usual and saw her hurriedly place something under her seat cushion.

But even then I didn't make the connection. I guess it's true what they say: The writer is always the last to know. Maybe I didn't *want* to know.

Finally, though, I'd had it up to here with the lies, the deception, the furtive rustling of pages at all hours, the whispered phone conversations about structure and plot.

I decided to confront her right then and there. "Let's get it out in the open," I said. "You're reading someone else. WHO IS HE? WHO'S THE HACK?"

For an instant, her face drained of color. Then the whole sordid tale came tumbling out. "Yes, yes," she confessed, "it's all true. God forgive me." Indeed, she *was* reading another man.

It was Garrison Keillor.

The news hit me like a two-by-four across the face. Garrison Keillor? Oh, don't get me wrong. The man is an OK writer. He had a bestseller a few years back with that kitschy *Lake Wobegone Days*. But my God! He's almost twice her age.

"What is it?" I said. "His long, clean flowing sentences? The allegorical references that pepper his prose? The constant use of a mythical Minnesota town as a metaphor for paradise lost?"

By now the tears were streaming down my cheeks, not that I should be unburdening myself to you, you have your own problems.

"I thought you liked a clipped, epigrammatic style," I sobbed.

"Set-up, punchline, set-up, punchline. I thought that's what you wanted."

"It's not that," she said. "It has nothing to do with writing style."

"THEN FOR GOD'S SAKE, WHAT IS IT?" I screamed.

When she spoke again, it was in a voice barely above a whisper.

"He's just... funnier than you are."

So there it was, out in the open.

She was reading someone who made her laugh, who made her feel younger, who took her back to the days before 24-hour comedy on cable, when you couldn't find a stand-up in every gin joint in town.

There were so many things I could have told her about Garrison Keillor, but what was the use?

Would it make any difference if she knew the guy was so out of it that he doesn't even use a word processor? That he writes on a battered old Smith Corona with an "r" key that sticks and a left margin indicator that hasn't worked since the Watergate scandal?

Or that he's an absolutely atrocious speller? The editors at the *New Yorker* say the guy has about 20 "problem" words — you know, those words we misspell over and over no matter how many times we use them? Cincinnati is one of his. He always spells it with two "t"s.

So, that's where things stand as of this writing. Sure, we've thought about counseling. There's a contemporary lit professor over at Johns Hopkins who's read all the current humorists: Keillor, Roy Blount Jr., P.J. O'Rourke, Buchwald.

"Let's go talk to him," I said. "Let's see if we can save this relationship."

But she wouldn't listen. All I heard was Garrison Keillor this and Garrison Keillor that. To rub salt in the wound, she added a breathless account of the day he was autographing his new book in Washington and the two of them struck up a conversation, the gist of which was: "My pen ran dry. Do you have an extra?"

"What's the use of counseling?" she said. "I'll only read the guy again. Maybe it's better if we arrive at some sort of understanding. You read who *you* want, I'll read who *I* want."

So, apparently what we have going now is an open marriage. She doesn't even try to hide it anymore. If she sees a Dave Barry column in the paper, she'll read it right in front of me, as if I'm not even there.

Sometimes she even clips other humor columns from newspapers and magazines and sends them along to friends with the notation: "This guy is funny!"

The word "funny" is always underlined three times. *In red ink.*

Happy holidays, indeed.

How to tell when it's over

I got dumped for the first time in a small Italian restaurant in lower Manhattan, to which she had summoned me with the cryptic message: "We have to talk."

A few minutes after the eggplant parmigiana arrived at our table, she suddenly put down her fork.

"It's all over between us," she said quietly.

"What are you trying to say?" I asked.

"We're through," she said. "You and I are history."

"Listen," I said, "if there's something on your mind, just spit it out."

"I don't want to go out with you any more," she said. "We're finished."

"God, I hate when you act so *mysterious!*" I said. "Get to the point, will you?"

The woman was trying to tell me something, but for the life of me, I couldn't figure out what it was. All this double-talk and gobbledygook of hers was driving me crazy.

Then, about 20 minutes later, just as the dessert cart rumbled away and I took my first bite of an absolutely delicious cannoli, it hit me: My God! This woman was ending our relationship!

She was saying that it was all over between us! That we were through! That she didn't want to go out with me anymore!

Why she couldn't have said all that in the first place was beyond me.

Anyway, as I walked slowly back to my apartment that night, with a steady rain falling on the darkened streets and a tugboat sounding mournfully in the distance, one thought consumed me above all others: Wasn't $22.95 a little steep for eggplant parmigiana?

I mean, I could understand if it were the veal piccata or the house specialty, that seafood dish with the lobster and shrimp and everything.

But 23 bucks for eggplant? I'm sorry, that's highway robbery. You might as well wear a ski mask and wave a gun in front of your customers if you're charging prices like those.

I bring up this ugly incident after all these years not because the price of eggplant has shot through the roof (it hasn't), but because of the recent proliferation of books and TV talk shows centered on one common theme: How to tell if your relationship has gone sour.

Here are one man's warning signs:
- She calls you Ken when your name is Kevin.
- When you gently remind her of that fact, she snarls: "Ken, Kevin... what's the big deal? Boy, isn't it just like you to nitpick!"
- She says "We never do anything anymore" and quickly adds, "Not that that's such a bad thing."
- She begs out of dates by explaining that "MacGyver" is on tonight.
- When you call, she barks into the phone that the police have telephone monitoring equipment "to stop this sort of harassment."
- When you call back, she squeezes her nose with her fingers and says in a disembodied voice: "We're sorry, the number you have reached is not in service at this time..."
- Finally, she says "We have to talk" and picks a pricey restaurant before you can blurt out: "Bob's Big Boy, 7:30."
- She begins the conversation at the restaurant by saying: "I'll start with the jumbo shrimp cocktail."
- She continues the conversation by saying: "They have a terrific imported wine list here."
- Midway through the entree, she says: "Ken, it's not you, it's me."
- Quickly she adds: "No, come to think of it, it's you."
- For the next ten minutes, she proceeds to tick off your many failings, chief among them "this hang-up you have about names."
- If you raise your voice even slightly to defend yourself, she hisses: "For God's sake, Ken, let's not have a scene here!"
- She says she hasn't "grown" in the relationship, even though between her appetizer, eggplant parmigiana, side order of pasta and half a loaf of bread, you'd swear she was growing right before your eyes.
- She says the two of you "can still be friends, although friends don't necessarily have to *see* each other, right?"
- When the dessert cart rumbles by, she sings out: "Diet, schmiet. How's the strawberry cheesecake tonight, Vito?"
- She says "I've found someone else" and you notice she's holding hands with the busboy.
- When the check arrives, she gives you a firm handshake and says "Have a nice life, Ken" before sprinting for the exit.

"Kevin!" you yell. "The name's Kevin!"

Not that it does any good at this point.

Hairdo comes with many don'ts

I'll tell you what Nancy and I can't talk about without a huge fight: her hair.

Hair sounds like an innocuous subject, right? Like the weather? Something you can kick around without anyone getting all huffy and stomping out of the room? Hah! Don't try it. Really. It's just not worth it.

Here's what I mean. Nancy comes home the other day, right? I hear the car pull in the driveway and I look out the window and there she is. And then I notice something that just chills me to the bone. She's had something done to her hair.

"Mother of God!" I whisper, and now I start freaking out and running around in circles and thinking: "What do I do?! What do I do?!"

Because I *know* what's coming. I can almost hear the bell for Round 1.

So I run to the back of the house, because my plan is to run out the back door and hide in the woods. Only the back door is locked, so I try a window, but as soon as I get the window open, Nancy is... I'm telling you, this woman should be a Green Beret or something.

Because somehow she's covered 40 yards of rough terrain in the span of five seconds. And now she's standing right there as I pop the screen and crawl out the window.

"What do you think?" she says. She's pointing to her hair.

"It's very nice," I say.

This is what I always say about her hair. It's a conditioned response. It's the only response that's *safe*. In the most literal sense of the word.

She once asked what I thought of a new hairstyle and I said: "Well..."

That's all I said. Just: "Well..."

I didn't say: "Well, it's OK."

I didn't say: "Well, I'm not so sure about this one."

All I said was: "Well..." Because I was still making up my mind, right? And she got all annoyed. You would have thought I said: "Well, that's why they have hats."

We had a big fight that time. She accused me of being insensitive. And I said... well, never mind what *I* said. But I learned my lesson.

So this time I use common sense and I say: "It's very nice."

But she just keeps staring at me, like she can see into my brain or something. And finally she says: "You don't like it."

"Yes, I *do*," I say.

"No, you don't," she says. "I can tell."

Well, the truth is her haircut is just OK. It's got this... *flip* in the front.

But I can't tell her that.

Because if I say something like: "That flip in the front... I don't know," she's going to get hot. I've seen it a hundred times. And then we'll be having this 12-round, Ali-Frazier dustup right there in front of the kids.

Besides, it's not just the flip. The whole thing is a little too short. But that's just my opinion. A hairstyle is such a subjective thing.

Look, I understand the *pain* behind a haircut. It's an emotional experience, no question. There's a loss of control there. You're sitting in that chair and someone is hovering over you, snipping and snipping, and it's like your whole identity is being... altered.

So now she says: "Do you know how much I spent for this haircut?"

I never know what to say when she asks me this. One time I took a guess and said: "$27.50?"

And the answer was 60 bucks. I mean, I wasn't even in the ballpark.

So this time, when she asks if I know how much her haircut cost, I say: "No, how much?"

"It was very expensive," she says.

So all I say is: "Maybe if you blow it out..."

Because that's what she says to me all the time, right? She comes home with a new haircut and says: "You'll like it when I blowdry it."

But this time I say: "Maybe if you blow it out ..." and she stomps away. All huffy.

I don't know. There's no sense in talking about hair with some people. Honestly. It's not worth the aggravation.

But now *I* start to feel bad because I know *she* feels bad. So I walk into the kitchen. And she's rustling in the knife drawer, which is always a bad sign, only this time she pulls out a potato peeler.

So now she starts furiously peeling these potatoes and there's potato skin flying all over the place and it's sort of hard to concentrate.

"Look," I say, "What I meant is..."

"Hah!" she says. "What you *meant!*"

"What I meant was..."

"Lemme tell you something," she says. "I like my hair. And that's all that counts."

"Absolutely," I say.

I probably should have said that in the first place. But you never know how that'll go over.

Your trash, my treasures

It all started when we decided to get rid of some junk in the attic, and she tossed my Mickey Mantle autograph baseball glove in the trash.

"What are you doing?" I said.

"Throwing out this junk," she said. "We've got a lot of junk up here."

"That's not junk," I said. "That's a Mickey Mantle autograph glove. I got it when I was ten. You can't throw that out."

"You haven't picked up that glove in years," she said. "And who's Mickey Mantle anyway?"

"I can't believe I'm hearing this," I said. "Who's *Mickey Mantle?* Maybe the greatest baseball player in history, that's who."

"Well," she said, "he's dead now. So what difference does it make?"

"Mickey Mantle's not dead," I said. "You're thinking of Billy Martin. Or Dean Martin."

"Dean Martin's not dead," she said. "You're thinking of Sammy Davis, Jr."

"Listen," I said, "we're not throwing out my old baseball glove. If you want to get rid of some junk, what about those old photographs?"

"Those are our wedding pictures," she said. "You want to throw out our wedding pictures?!"

"Let me tell you something about wedding pictures," I said. "Nobody ever looks at wedding pictures. Wedding pictures have the same shelf life as a quart of milk. They should come with an expiration date. Three, four days after they're taken, you might as well toss 'em."

"You're nuts," she said. "People look at their wedding pictures all the time."

"Well," I said, "I'd rather not look at our wedding pictures. We had some shaky-looking characters at our wedding. The dance floor looked like the exercise yard at Attica."

"We had a very nice wedding," she said. "If you don't count the groom's friends."

"Look," I said, "let's not argue about my friends. Let me just say this: Suppose we had a party and we said to the guests, 'OK, what do you want to see, a Mickey Mantle autograph baseball glove or some old wedding pictures?' People would want to see the glove. You can take that to the bank."

"No," they wouldn't, she said. "No one would want to see that stupid glove, I don't care how much they were drinking."

"Yes, they would," I said. "It's an *objet d'art*. Personally signed by the Mick. And you wanted to toss it in the garbage. With the coffee grinds. And orange peels. Unbelievable."

"Give me a break," she said. "It's not the cloth they used to wrap Gandhi's body."

"Before we continue with this cleaning project," I said, "we better get something straight. What's your definition of junk?"

"Junk?" she said. "Junk is an old baseball glove with some dead guy's name on it."

"He's not dead," I said. "How many times do we have to go over this? The guy lives in Dallas or something. Mickey Mantle. I can't believe you've never heard of Mickey Mantle."

"I don't want to talk about it any more," she said. "And what about these old Elvis posters? I happen to know for a fact that Elvis is dead."

"Lots of people would argue that," I said. "I know a woman who says The King works at a Shoe Town in Cincinnati. You better save those posters. But let's get rid of those old photo albums."

"Those are my baby pictures," she said. "You want to throw away my baby pictures?"

"What is it with you and old pictures anyway?" I said. "You have stock in Kodak or something? Besides, if you've seen one baby, you've seen them all."

"I'm glad you didn't go into pediatrics," she said. "But these old books have *got* to go."

"Those are my old college textbooks," I said. "Look, here's a Hemingway anthology."

"Hemingway," she said. "Great. Another dead guy."

"The man's writing lives on," I said. "You just hate every author whose name isn't Stephen King."

"Let me tell you something about Stephen King," she said. "I've met Stephen King. I've read all of Stephen King's books. Believe me, Hemingway was no Stephen King."

"Why?" I said. "Because he didn't churn out a novel every five minutes? Hemingway won the Pulitzer *and* the Nobel Prize for Literature. What did Stephen King ever win — the Satanists' Seal of Approval?"

"I don't want to talk about Stephen King," she said. "Let's get back to work here."

"That set of weights stays," I said.

"Don't touch that exercise bike," she said.

"We're not tossing those old *Life* magazines," I said.

"Leave that old suitcase," she said.

I'm sure glad we finally got the attic straightened out.

You gotta love the '90s Guy

Sensitive is out.

That's probably the best news for the '90s Guy — if you don't count the fact that more and more women are willing to split the check.

Which isn't to say the '90s Guy is unfeeling. No sir. If he's driving with the wife and kids and they hit a dog, the '90s Guy doesn't shrug and say "Hey, that's what they have kennels for," before draining his orange Big Gulp and letting out a burp that can be heard in the next area code.

By the same token, the '90s Guy doesn't take long walks amid the brilliant autumn foliage, only to collapse on a rock with tears streaming down his face and say: "It's just so... *beautiful*."

The face of the '90s Guy doesn't cloud over with concern when Hope has her baby on "thirtysomething." (Whether the '90s Guy even watches "thirtysomething" is open to debate. Statistics indicate that on Tuesday evenings at precisely ten o'clock, trillions of American men head for the basement to sandpaper and varnish old bureaus. They return promptly at eleven.)

Is the '90s guy supportive? Understanding? Good to his mom? Does he floss? Yeah, yeah, yeah. You betcha.

The '90s Guy knows day care *and* the Dolphins. He can handle ATMs and Arsenio, call waiting and computer dating, safe sex, Tex-Mex and Comtrex, Bud Light and the Berenstain Bears. He can speak eloquently on the subject of recycling as well as relief pitching.

He's just not such a... *dork* about things, the way he was in the '80s.

The '90s Guy doesn't push the sleeves of his sport coat up to his elbows. He doesn't "relate" to anyone. He understands that Lamaze is a huge con game, because all the breathing in the world is no substitute for 750 cc's of morphine when a 7-lb, 11-oz baby is careening down the birth canal of the woman he loves.

The '90s Guy accepts the ground rules of modern romance: No fooling around on the first date, casual exchange of sexual histories on the second date, a more frank and detailed examination of sexual biographies on the third date, an open and honest discussion of morality and sexual inclinations on the fourth date, the exchange of blood test results on the fifth date, the engagement of private detective surveillance on the sixth date, the joint analysis of polygraph data on the seventh date, followed by — tadaaa! — wild, spontaneous sex (with a brief time out for the fitting of a condom) on the eighth date.

Hell, yes, the '90s Guy understands all that. And has no problem with any of it. He is, above everything else, flexible.

When the auto industry lost its very soul and sold out to the Japanese, and big roomy Chrysler Imperials gave way to Chevy Chevettes with all the leg room of the Apollo 12, the '80s Guy adjusted his lovemaking by disdaining the back seat of his car in favor of cheap motels with short-stay rates and lava lamps in the rooms.

So it is with the '90s Guy. He knows the old line "If you really loved me, you'd do it" has no more relevance today than saying "I like Ike" or "Oswald acted alone."

There is disease out there. The '90s Guy is no fool, even though he feels like one at times, such as when he tries to program the VCR to record (there are only two or three '90s Guys in the whole world who can do this) or when he confesses to not understanding "Twin Peaks."

What else can we say about the '90s Guy? Here's something: He's very big on communicating. The genesis for this occurred some years ago, when the '80s Woman turned to the '80s Guy (probably during the NBA finals) and said: "You know what your problem is? You don't *communicate*."

So the '80s Guy started communicating — although not without first looking up the word in the dictionary. Pretty soon he was telling her about his hopes, his fears, his dreams, his new riding mower with the attachable leaf-raker, his agonizing over whether it was less filling or tasted great, until finally the '80s Woman rolled her eyes to heaven and thought: "Geez, this guy just won't SHUT UP!"

Well, guess what? The '90s Guy won't shut up, either. Ask him the time, he'll tell you who made the watch. In other words, it feels so good to unburden himself that the '90s Guy has turned into a loose-lipped, swivel-hipped, chattering fool, although to be honest many of his deepest thoughts center on the Jeep Cherokee — would I look cool driving that baby or what?

In the next column: How to tell if you're a '90s Guy... providing you're man (or woman) enough to read it.

Looking for love in the personals

Recently I thumbed through the personal ads of a yuppie magazine to see what was new in the exciting world of romance.

I myself am not in the market for a relationship, being somewhat involved right now with a wife and two children who don't stop moving unless you drop a net on them and use a tranquilizer gun.

I might be interested in a stress management seminar, but not a girlfriend.

But the personal ads are the most entertaining reading in any of these modern living magazines that cater to the Volvo and brie set.

Sensitive, caring DWF seeks SWM with same qualities. No smokers, or I'll kill you.

Warm SBM seeks SBF for dining, theater, travel. Prefer you pick up check.

Adventuresome MJM seeks daring JF for discreet, degrading rendezvous in sleazy motel, some sewing.

Oh, it's great stuff. I recommend it highly, especially if you've had it up to here with articles such as "600 Ways to Serve Pasta on a Bed of Leaves!" or "We Rate the Hottest Restaurants of the Sinai Peninsula!"

The first thing you notice about the personal ads is that everyone who advertises is attractive. Or so he or she says.

Everyone is tall and handsome. Or trim and pretty. Everyone has sparkling blue eyes like Paul Newman. Or a drop-dead figure like Vanna White.

I don't know what happens to ugly people, but they sure don't advertise in the personals. Maybe they take out ads in *Troll* ("The magazine for beastly looking folks.")

Just once, I would like to see a personal that read:

"Chubby, Hunchback of Notre Dame-type, only with worse complexion, seeks stout woman with a face like a bulldog's and overbite, for romance, possible commitment. Suggest we don't have children."

Even plain-looking people don't advertise in the personals.

You never see ads like:

"*5-foot-9 guy with spare tire, bags under eyes, not much of a chin, looks like your grocer, seeks woman who's put on a few pounds, doesn't use makeup and wears thick glasses. Would prefer your hair be pulled back as well.*"

Another thing about the personals: Everyone who advertises is athletic. Everyone jogs, enjoys racquetball, swimming, weight-lifting, archery, skiing.

My only question is: Do any of these people work? If you're spending all your time playing beer-league softball, I have to figure there's not a whole lot of disposable income in that household.

Besides, why would two jocks hook up for a date? The tandem would never stop moving. The only time you two could talk would be during a timeout in your one-on-one basketball game. Even then you'd spend the time guzzling Gatorade and toweling each other off.

The point is, you never see an ad from someone who likes to lie around and vegetate, such as:

"*Disinterested lout who sprawls in Barcalounger eating Cheese Nips and watching moronic cop shows seeks sluggish woman with own snack supply to do same. Serious inquiries only.*"

Another thing about the personals: everyone who advertises loves to travel.

Everyone enjoys ski vacations in Vail, cruises to the Caribbean, jetting off to Europe — even in this age of planes dropping out of the sky because the mechanic with the rivet-gun was nursing a hangover.

What about the stay-at-home types? What about the folks who think a run to the bowling alley is a big night? Don't *they* use the personals?

Apparently not, because you never see ads such as:

"*Xenophobic woman who found local state fair too fast and prefers to stay in living room and knit pot holders seeks middle-aged man with unconquerable fear of flying to learn origami. Could lead to relationship, providing we don't wander off my block.*"

Also, in the personals, everyone is personable, vivacious and energetic. Everyone enjoys life to the fullest, and loves to laugh.

In fact, these people seem so well-adjusted that any normal person would loathe them the minute they read their ads.

Me, I think there has to be a place for those poor schnooks with personality problems to advertise:

"*Severely withdrawn individual, distant, one of those look-at-me-and-I'll-cry sorts, seeks timid woman with wallflower personality for company. I can't even envision a normal relationship. But we'll spend afternoons full of long silences, averting our eyes, stammering and staring off into space. No closet gregarious types, please.*"

If you're a disturbed loner, I don't see how you ignore an ad like that.

Dear confused: Get counseling

Dear Ann Landers:

I am dating a terrific man. So what's the problem? "Bob" won't tell me anything about himself, even his last name. I don't know where he lives or works.

Every night, we meet at my apartment, where I fix him dinner and we have sex. Then he goes home. When he calls me, he's always whispering. Sometimes I hear children playing in the background.

Then there's this: He wears a small gold band on his left ring finger. He says the ring was given to him by a fraternal order. When I ask him the name of the organization, he says he "can't remember."

Ann, what do you make of his strange behavior? — Confused in Columbus, Ohio.

Dear Confused:

"Bob" sounds like a great catch. Your suspicious nature borders on paranoia. I suggest you go for counseling.

Dear Ann Landers:

Some years ago, you printed a wonderful article that touched me unlike anything I had ever read before. It was about how if you work real hard or something, then... well, I forget the rest. Or else it was about the value of friendship. Or it had something to do with raising kids.

Anyway, I clipped that article and pinned it to my refrigerator with one of those fruit magnets. It stayed there for seven years. Then, a few weeks ago, I went on a bender and didn't come home for two days. Apparently the dog got so hungry that he jumped up and ate the clipping.

I was so mad! It didn't seem enough to shout "Bad doggie!" so I had "Bucky" put to sleep. That was a big mistake. I grew so lonely that I started combing the local pounds for a new dog. But "Bucky" was a pure white Samoyed, and where are you going to find one of those?

Ann, could you reprint that wonderful article? — Hopeful in Helena, Montana

Dear Hopeful:
"Bucky" sounds like he had a screw loose. So do you. I urge you to go for counseling.

Dear Ann Landers:
My fiance and I get along fine except for a couple of things. "Eve" keeps calling me "jerko," "fruitcake," "loser," etc. Every time I try to kiss her, she elbows me away and shouts: "Dammit, I'm *trying* to watch TV." At cocktail parties, whenever I talk to somebody, she stands behind me and rolls her eyes and makes little circles around her temple with her index finger. I've whirled around and caught her doing this many times.

Counting gifts, Broadway tickets, dinners at expensive restaurants, the down payment on her car and the engagement ring, I have spent about $10,000 on "Eve" over the past six months. The only thing she gave me was a lousy Hallmark card on my birthday that said: "Congratulations! It's a baby boy!"

Am I being overly sensitive? — Moping in Manhattan
Dear Moping:
You approach a relationship with a great deal of unrealistic expectations. I implore you to go for counseling.

Dear Ann Landers:
I am so hurt. My sister is getting married in three months. Yesterday, we received an invitation to the wedding, on which was scrawled in ballpoint pen: "No Gypsies!"

Ann, my husband "Drazen" is a Gypsy. We had planned to take his small horse-drawn cart to the ceremony and perhaps do a little fortune-telling, herbal healing and knife sharpening.

Now I don't know what to do. — Anguished in Akron, Ohio
Dear Anguished:
For the sake of family unity, go to the wedding by yourself. Have you and your husband thought about counseling?

Dear Ann Landers:

You were dead wrong in your answer to "Doing Time in Texas," the woman who smothered her husband with a plastic bag after he spent the whole weekend watching football on TV.

I agree: the fat slob had it coming. But to suggest, as you did, that his body should have been fed to the wolves struck me as a bit much. — Disagreeing in Dallas

Dear Disagreeing:

I heard from about 10,000 other readers who expressed the same opinion. I urge <u>all</u> of you to get counseling.

Dear Ann Landers:

You're always telling people: "Go for counseling, go for counseling."

Has it ever occurred to you that some people simply can't afford counseling? —Boiling Mad in Miami

Dear Boiling:

Toots, you've got a chip on your shoulder the size of Mount McKinley. I urge you especially to go for counseling.

Fun & Games in the '90s

Last call at the 7-Eleven

Recently I had the opportunity to dine at the 7-Eleven on U.S. 20, next to Ken's Custom Car Stereo and the Hair Loft. Here is my report:

We arrived at a little past 1:30 in the morning, and so had the place virtually to ourselves, with the exception of a swarthy, tattooed fellow who was mumbling incoherently to himself near the "Test Your Blood Pressure" machine.

As an appetizer, I chose the medium-size Slim Jim, while my companion opted for the Cheetos.

Although it took several minutes to unravel the plastic wrapping, the Slim Jim had a spicy "smoked" quality to it, with a chewiness that was at first oddly refreshing and then mildly exasperating.

My companion, on the other hand, reported that the Cheetos seemed "stale," perhaps owing to a gaping hole we later found in the plastic bag.

A good order of Cheetos has a characteristic texture to it, made all the more tempting when the orange food coloring rubs off on your fingers and you have to lick them clean. These, sadly, had none of the Cheetos "snap," which we attempted to point out to the maitre d', who was wearing a bored expression at the cash register while browsing through the latest issue of *Biker Girls*.

It taught us a valuable lesson, however: When dining out on Cheetos, it is best to select a bag from the display rack, instead of picking one up willy-nilly off the floor.

As an entree, I decided to go with the 1/4-pound "Big Bite" hot dog, which I was told was the latest entry in 7-Eleven's glittering array of "fun" foods.

This prompted the following conversation with the maitre d', who quickly dropped his sullen countenance in favor of a veneer of quiet professionalism:

"Want anything on that?"

"Mustard's fine. Maybe a little sauerkraut. Little chilly out there tonight."

"That right?"

"Yeah."

My companion elected to pass up the heat'n'eat Italian sub sandwich in favor of the Hormel chili, served in a plastic container and heated in the handy microwave oven, which was located under the brightly colored sign proclaiming: "Carton cigarettes - $12.89."

"You ask me, the Dinty Moore stew's better in the microwave," the maitre d' informed my companion, touching off a spirited debate about the legendary lumberjack-turned-canned-food-mogul.

We had hoped to enjoy a bottle of inexpensive wine with our meal, something from the Blue Nun line or perhaps from the Bartles&Jaymes or Seagrams collections of fine wine coolers. But as this was not possible due to local liquor ordinances, I chose a can of the Mountain Dew.

The bubbly concoction was thoroughly predictable, if a little too sweet for my taste, evoking images of bygone TV commercials featuring a group of carefree youngsters swinging on ropes and splashing into a cool mountain stream. My companion went with the orange Super Slurpee, which was self-served from a set of high-pressure valves in the rear of the store, near the bags of Kingsford charcoal.

Soon it was time for coffee, and, as we did not see the dessert cart rumbling anywhere nearby, we went off in search of something for our sweet tooth.

I chose the Hostess Twinkies, the legendary twin mounds of moist cake filled with a fluffy core of white stuff.

My companion also chose an old favorite, the Yodels, gentle swirls of cream in a soft chocolate shell. Soon, she lapsed into what experienced restaurant critics call "sugar overload" as the Yodels reacted with the Super Slurpee, producing the craving to either bang one's head against the wall or do laps around the parking lot.

As we lingered over dessert, we noticed that the store seemed to be filling up, and we were informed that it was nearing 2 a.m. and "the bars are closing."

Indeed, some of the new arrivals seemed quite animated, with one unsteady patron spilling a bag of Fritos corn chips onto the floor and touching off peals of hysterical laughter from his four companions.

We played one quick game of "Ninja Warrior" on the video machine, after which we weaved our way between two hollow-eyed bikers and headed out into the parking lot.

Altogether, it was a very different dining experience. *Total cost of the meal*: a very reasonable $6.79, excluding the 50 cents for "Ninja Warrior," which was a rip-off anyway since the leg kick button didn't even work.

I gave it two stars.

The search for Spandex people

It was a few years ago when the Spandex People first began appearing in public dressed in their body stockings and what have you.

Like most Americans, I kept waiting for the Spandex People to go away. But whether through over-breeding, great strides in medical science or 20 percent discount sales at Herman's and the Athletic Attic, they have seemingly multiplied like rabbits, until you can barely walk down the street today without encountering one or two of the species.

What should be obvious by now — but apparently isn't to some of the Spandex People — is that Spandex is a fabric not flattering to everyone.

That is to say, unless you weigh 110 pounds and have the same robust appetite as a sparrow, it would probably be best for all concerned if you eschewed Spandex in favor of a more, um, loose-fitting garment, such as that old "I'm With Stupid" sweatshirt picked up at Al's T-Shirt Emporium on the boardwalk.

Now, I know what you're thinking.

You're thinking: My, my... what's behind his latest screed on Spandex?

Simmering jealousy?

Thinly veiled resentment that I don't have the kind of sleek, whipcord-tough body that looks smashing in Spandex?

A cancerous envy directed at the legions of trim, hard-bodied, rosy-cheeked dudes and dudettes who look absolutely stunning in Spandex?

Sure, there *could* be some of that at work here. I'm not above a good old-fashioned public display of petulance over the body God gave me (and Burger King, Sarah Lee and Budweiser destroyed).

In fact, let me be even *more* up front and admit to once owning my very own pair of cool ultra-tight bicycle shorts.

They were given to me as a gift by a relative, who had apparently mistaken me for a seventh-grader, albeit one who shaves regularly and is married.

Either that or this relative was under the impression that I had recently concluded a six-month juice fast for religious purposes and was now down to my fighting trim of, oh, 87 pounds or so.

Anyway, I tried on the bicycle shorts and they certainly looked cool — at least if your definition of cool squares with mine.

They fit great in the thighs (he said modestly). They fit great in the hips (he said with only the faintest hint of a blush).

And they fit great in the waist — if you overlooked (and I don't see how you could) THE HUGE ROLL OF FLAB THAT HUNG OVER THE G@#$%¢&* WAISTBAND!!

I myself could not overlook the huge roll of flab that hung over the waistband. This was because I was standing in front of a mirror at the time, and each glance into it caused me to recoil in horror, as one would if suddenly discovering the presence of a third eyeball in the center of one's forehead.

(Note: Many of the Spandex People apparently don't have mirrors in their homes, but fortunately we have several — two of them full-length — in ours.)

In any event, the sight of me decked out in bicycle shorts was disturbing indeed. I'm glad the children weren't home, as even a quick glimpse could have scarred them for life. Say what you will about Post-Traumatic Stress Disorders, but it's prolonged exposure to ugliness such as has been described here that drives adults, never mind innocent children, into therapy.

My reaction to the sight of me in Spandex?

Oh, I guess pretty much what you'd expect — which was to quickly take off the bicycle shorts, start a roaring, gasoline-stoked fire in a barrel, and incinerate those suckers into a pile of ashes, all the while chanting: "Spandex is the devil's tool... Spandex is the devil's tool..."

At one time, of course, the Spandex People were more or less confined to gyms, health spas and yogurt bars, where the government could monitor their activities and decent citizens could, for the most part, avoid them.

Now, however, the Spandex People are allowed to roam freely, enjoying many of the same constitutional liberties as you or I (assuming *you* don't wear the stuff, too).

I myself have spotted the Spandex People at church functions, Tupperware parties, street fairs, even PTA meetings.

Now you say to yourself: What kind of sick, demented soul would wear Spandex to a PTA meeting?

And *why*? Just to show off a perfectly taut body, complete with washboard stomach and rippling muscles, while the parents and teachers discuss a new vending machine for the teacher's lounge?

My point exactly.

Not that I'm bitter.

Although, let's face it, I have every right to be.

A workout to die for

I watch them hurry in the door, flashing their gold membership cards and swinging their $70 Nike gear bags, a grim look on their faces as they stride purposefully to the carpeted locker rooms.

I am at The Health Club.

It's time for The Workout.

God help us all.

Stairmaster, free weights, Lifecycle… is this what it's all about?

Racquetball, Nautilus… whatever happened to a couple of beers after work?

In the weight room, sculpted bodies grunt and strain under the harsh fluorescent light. Huge men with wide leather belts lift enormous amounts of metal. People check themselves in the mirror. Man, you see that monster in the Oklahoma shirt? He's really *ripped*!

Lats, abs, pecs… you work out here often? Really? How come I've never seen you here before? My name's Steve, what's yours? Bambi? Nice to meet you, Bambi.

Bambi, Bambi… didn't you use to tend bar at Christophers?

I walk by the membership desk. A trim young man in Reebok sweats and regulation Hitler Youth Corps haircut is droning: "…only the finest in equipment and facilities. Our instructors are certified in CPR. With our Executive-Plus membership, you pay just…"

The two women he's talking to wear eager, bouncy expressions. I want to scream "GET OUT! SAVE YOURSELVES WHILE YOU STILL CAN!" But it's too late. They have The Fever. You can see it in their eyes.

Step aerobics, accelerated aerobics, Jazzercise… I saw a woman pass out in dance aerobics once.

They threw a bucket of cold water on her and dragged her to her feet. Valerie, the gaunt, pinch-faced instructor — think of spike-shoed Rosa Klebb in "From Russia With Love" — slapped her hard across the face. Then everyone shrieked: "Angela, you're *slowing* down the class!"

No, not really. But it *could* happen. These are dangerously single-minded people here. Nothing must interfere with The Workout.

What is this, Wednesday? Upper-body work. I strap myself into the cold steel of the Torquemada-approved shoulder machine. One, two, one, two... that's enough of that. It's Miller time.

I wander over to the racquetball courts. The air crackles with intensity. The familiar *THWOCK! THWOCK*! of the ball echoes everywhere. So do horrible screams and violent oaths. It's like being in the bowels of a Turkish prison.

A small man with terrier-like determination is on Court 2. He yells to his partner: "Next time I'll drill ya in the head!"

Later, Sam, his partner, tells me: "My doctor says racquetball is good for stress."

Right. But not when you play the heir-apparent to Mark David Chapman. I tell Sam to memorize the term "walking time bomb" for the day his partner finally snaps and guns down three people in the locker room. The media will be all over this place.

The Club is crowded now. Snatches of conversation can be heard over the variety- rock blaring from the speakers. The talk is of cholesterol levels, blood pressure readings, MRI results.

A man says: "You want my orthopedist's number? Best elbow man in town."

Some poor fool lit up a Salem at the juice bar not long ago. A crowd quickly gathered and beat him to death with their bare hands, punching and stomping him until the walls were flecked with blood. After that, they paraded his body around while everyone raised cans of Carbo 2000 and roared in appreciation.

No, not really. But it *could* happen. This is Peking at the height of the Cultural Revolution. The Red Guard of the '90s permit only one vice. "Make Your Body Beautiful." This concludes a brief message from Chairman Mao.

I walk by the tanning salon. Men and women with milky, dead-of-winter skin shuffle lemming-like into the booths, only to emerge with that pinkish, pre-cancerous glow.

A staff member ("Hi! I'm Teri!"), with a serious two-months-in-Barbados tan, spots me. She flashes the requisite Health Club smile and chirps: "We have a three o'clock available..."

No, no, I was just... a man lost his life on the rubberized indoor track yesterday. Apparently he wasn't moving quite fast enough for the fast-track young executive behind him, wired from seventeen cups of coffee and a heady afternoon of mergers and acquisitions. The police termed the trampling an "accident," even though the man's body was subsequently run over by 32 different pairs of running shoes.

No, no. It didn't happen. But, believe me, it *could* happen.

None of that concerns me now. I lie spent and exhausted in front of the big-screen TV.

The Workout is over. I feel much, much better.

Smoke on the water? Not here!

Commercial, 30 seconds, "Maryland is Breathin' Easy!" campaign.

(Video: Dawn on the Chesapeake Bay. A seagull glides lazily over the waves. The sun rises majestically behind a lighthouse. Watermen lift teeming baskets of crabs onto the decks of a workboat.)
(Music is light, airy.)
Announcer: "There's a place on the Eastern Shore..."
(Aerial shot of colonial-era church with white steeple.)
"Where the seafood is the best in the world!"
(Huge table is heaped with oysters, clams, etc.)
"But if you come to Maryland..."
(Shot of smiling family in late-model automobile; Mom studies map.)
"There're two things you should know:"
(Inner Harbor is shown glittering at night.)
"No. 1, we'll treat you like royalty..."
(A beaming William Donald Schaefer waves from window of Governor's Mansion in Annapolis.)
"And No. 2, we *don't* cotton to smokers."
(Police SWAT team kicks in the door of a rowhouse; the wide-eyed resident frantically puts out a Marlboro and runs for a rear exit.)
"So whether you're watching the O's at Camden Yards..."
(Cal Ripken smacks a line-drive double off "no-smoking" warning; gives thumbs-up sign.)
"Or visiting the Baltimore zoo..."
(A baboon grimaces as smokers walk by.)
"Or having lunch at McDonald's..."
(Teen-age fry cook looks up, spots customer smoking, glares.)
"Our message is simple:"
(Fry cook hurriedly dials 911.)
"Don't light up!"
(Police arrive. Smoker is led out in handcuffs as other customers cheer.)

"Because in Maryland…"
(*Smiling fellow workers gather around fry cook and pat him on back.*)
"We care about your health!"
(*Fry cook receives commendation from mayor as proud parents look on.*)
"Sure, we're tough on smokers…"
(*Brooding shot of state penitentiary walls encircled by concertina wire.*)
"And getting even tougher."
(*Cell door clangs shut behind elderly man with hacking cough; man pleads for a Salem as guard sneers.*)
"We're considering some of the most rigorous anti-smoking bills in the country."
(*Shot of General Assembly in session.*)
"One bans smoking in the workplace."
(*Shivering smokers huddle outside office building as passers-by point and jeer.*)
"Another makes sure minors don't have access to cigarettes."
(*Man with mirrored sunglasses cruises middle-class neighborhood in sleek Cadillac, laughingly tossing cartons of cigarettes at pleading youngsters.*)
"One raises the tobacco tax 25 cents per pack."
(*Man is shown entering convenience store with two bags of gold. He leaves with a single carton of Winstons.*)
"One even bans cigarette vending machines!"
(*Mountains of battered, useless vending machines are strewn about a fetid landfill.*)
"Some call us far-thinking and visionary…"
(*Stirring shot of Stars and Stripes rippling in the breeze over Fort McHenry.*)
"While a few sourpusses might say we're repressive and dictatorial."
(*Old World War II footage of cheering fascists saluting Mussolini.*)
"We just think…"
(*A police cruiser screeches to a halt next to a church; man smoking outside is hustled away despite his protestations.*)

"There are better ways to enjoy yourself!"
(Shot of smiling family eating ice cream cones in park.)
"So if you come to Maryland..."
(Shot of milling crowds at Harborplace.)
"Do the right thing!"
(A man pulls a pack of cigarettes out of his pocket, shrugs, and tosses it in a trash can.)
"To ensure that your stay is pleasant..."
(Lone smoker on downtown bench is suddenly set upon by angry mob.)
"Leave that filthy habit at home!"
(As a smoker is pummeled viciously, a nearby cop nods and smiles.)
"This message brought to you..."
(Governor Schaefer gives A-OK sign.)
"By The Committee to Promote Maryland Tourism."
(Parting shots of Cal Ripken, Baltimore Mayor Kurt Schmoke, various watermen, hoteliers, restaurant owners and ordinary citizens smiling and waving.)

Let them eat cake, or else

Each time we have people over for dinner, the same conversation takes place during dessert with at least one pain-in-the-neck guest:

"How about a piece of cake?"

"Oh, I really shouldn't."

"Are you sure? It's very good. Maple walnut."

"Well, maybe just a sliver."

"Here you go..."

"Oh, God, that's too much. Half that."

"Coffee?"

"No, better not. It'll keep me up all night."

"Are you sure?"

"Well, maybe half a cup."

"Cream and sugar?"

"Doctor says I shouldn't "

"Are you sure?"

"Well, make it a smidgen of cream."

Let me say this to all you people who become health nuts when it comes time for dessert: I don't know what the hell a "sliver" is, OK?

And I don't know what a "smidgen" is.

Or a "tad." Or a "tidbit."

Or that thing — *especially* that thing — where you hold your thumb and forefinger about an inch apart and say: "Just *this* much."

These terms are not, so far as I know, listed on the Official Chart of Weights and Measures. If you want to use those goofy terms in the privacy of your own home — where, presumably, the other weirdos in your family are familiar with the lingo — fine, knock yourself out.

But *not* when I'm the guy wielding the cake cutter. Because all I want to know is: DO YOU WANT A !@#$%&* PIECE OF CAKE OR NOT?!

Sorry. It's just that... I don't know, it drives me nuts after a while. You ask a simple question and...

Here's the thing, too: People only act this way during dessert. You hardly ever hear anyone say during the main course: "Just a sliver of fried chicken for me, thanks," or "Oh, that's *way* too much broccoli; make it about half that."

And yet, as soon as the dessert arrives, people feel compelled to make life difficult for the host by suddenly remembering that they're watching their weight or avoiding caffeine or whatever.

A friend of mine dining in a steak house once put away a 16-oz. Porterhouse, a lobster, french fries, onion rings, a loaf of bread and four Coors. When the dessert cart rumbled up, he told the waiter: "Just a sliver of that pecan pie — I don't want to be a pig."

Another time, I was helping to serve cake at a birthday party when a woman said to me: "Honey, only a teeny-tiny-*teeny* piece for me."

So I gave her a piece the size of an M & M. Well. The woman gave me a dirty look and stomped away — although not before I wrestled my present from her grasp. (The gift turned out to be a nice sweater, too, robins-egg blue and just the right size. The woman was not cheap, I'll say that for her.)

But what does that mean, a "teeny-tiny-teeny piece?" It has to mean "extremely small," right? After all, that's two "teenys" (or "teenies") sandwiched around a "tiny."

As to the matter of coffee with dessert, this, too, has become an endless source of annoyance at the dinner table.

Listen, when I ask whether you want coffee, I don't want to hear your whole medical history, OK?

I don't want to hear that coffee keeps you up all night. Or that it makes you "jittery." Or that it makes you beat a path back and forth to the bathroom.

I'm not with the *New England Journal of Medicine*, OK? And I'm not here to kick around your bladder control problems with you.

All I want to know is: DO YOU WANT A !@#$%&* CUP OF COFFEE OR NOT?!

And what's with this "half a cup" business? If the stuff keeps you awake, try this: After the meal, go run eight miles with a 20-pound weight strapped to each ankle. Then, when you get home, drop to the floor and crank out 150 push-ups. Believe me, you'll be asleep in no time.

If that doesn't work, try throwing back a few shots of gin. My guess is you won't make it to "Nightline." Plus you'll enjoy a comfortable night's sleep, providing you haven't passed out in the kitchen sink or someplace like that and wake up with coffee grinds in your hair and your neck crooked at a 45-degree angle.

My point is, it would save us all a lot of time and trouble if you people would just eat the cake and drink the coffee.

OK?

Resuscitating party life

Not that many years ago, a successful party was measured by the number of people swilling beer from cowboy boots and lip-synching the words to "Louie, Louie" while attempting to lasso the family cocker spaniel with the drape cords.

Sadly, we are now in the era of the "New Sobriety." Not only is cocker-spaniel-roping frowned upon, but many parties consist of a half-dozen glum-looking people sipping mineral water and listlessly raking celery sticks through the low-cal spinach dip while talking about the leading economic indicators.

Sure, the cocker spaniels of this world can rest easier. But is this really the sort of *entertainment* we want after a tough week at the office? I think not.

The thing to remember is that nothing kills a party more effectively than dull guests, such as your earnest, young next-door neighbor who prattles on and on about his job at the shoe store.

Ignoring the glassy eyes of those around him, this fellow relates ad nauseum the most minute details of his job: where he keeps his shoe horn (right back pocket for ease of access), the many types of shoe trees available in his store, what polishes and leather-waterproofing compounds are "hot" right now, local celebrities (TV news anchors, ex-ballplayers) whose feet he has measured, etc.

Now, don't get me wrong. I'm sure it's all very interesting — to him. It's just that the shoe store "experience" is one that most of your guests are already familiar with, and one, quite frankly, that engenders a limited amount of curiosity.

Therefore, the smart host or hostess makes sure the room is dotted with a more eclectic mix of guests: Gypsies, circus clowns, tugboat skippers, former Nazis, Pee-Wee Herman, people who have had limbs amputated by sharks, and a parolee or two from the state penitentiary.

Nothing livens up a party better than a dead-eyed ex-con casually describing his last escape attempt, and how he was halfway through the ventilation shaft before the guards discovered him missing.

Gently urge him to detail the pandemonium that followed and how the bloodhounds, whipped into a frenzy by the musty scent of his sheets, finally tracked him to the prison pantry, where they found him cowering behind a 50-pound bag of rice.

By this point, a hushed semi-circle will have formed around your dangerous-looking friend, with all eyes riveted on the nasty, eight-inch scar on his neck, where a fellow con, out of his mind after inhaling cleaning fluid purloined from the janitorial crew, lunged at him with a shiv.

The shoe store clerk, on the other hand, will largely be ignored by your guests, even as he launches into an impassioned defense of arch supports as the ideal way to ward off painful heel spurs, stress fractures and the like.

This is probably neither here nor there, but another way to keep your guests happy is to steer clear of tiny plates.

I'm speaking here of those teensy-weensy paper plates that can comfortably hold *maybe* two chicken wings and a teaspoon of potato salad, necessitating an average of, oh, 24 trips to the buffet table to satisfy one's appetite.

By providing adult-sized plates, your guests will be so grateful that they'll usually leave your dog alone, instead of eyeing him longingly whenever there's a lull in the conversation.

One of the more vexing problems associated with entertaining is this: How does one gracefully get rid of guests at the end of the evening?

Let's face it, some people just don't know when to call it a night. There is no clear consensus on how to handle this, although running the vacuum cleaner under their feet in mid-conversation often sends a message that the party is winding to a close.

If this doesn't work, quietly excuse yourself for a few minutes. Then re-emerge in front of your guests wearing pajamas and a large, peaked nightcap, such as the type favored by Scandinavians during the long winter months.

In the unlikely event that your guest *still* doesn't take the hint, and continues forming his napkin into the shape of a noose and softly calling "Here, Spot! C'mere, boy!" more drastic action is called for.

Sharply poke your forefinger in his chest and bark: "You just don't *get* it, do you, (expletive)?!"

This more or less guarantees that people will be talking about your party for many weeks to come.

The dog won't soon forget what you did for him, either.

The manly art of male crying

Let me begin by saying that I'm not much of a crier myself, although given the right circumstances (bill for a new transmission, "Ol' Yeller" reruns, etc.), I can bawl like a baby.

Men first began crying openly in the late '70s, encouraged by the likes of Alan Alda and Phil Donahue, weepy guys with three-pack-a-day Kleenex habits who weren't afraid to show they were sensitive, vulnerable and so forth.

Women (at least some of them) seemed to go for this. So pretty soon you had a lot of guys with robin's-egg-blue leisure suits sobbing on women's shoulders during everything from foreign film presentations to the hatching of baby chicks.

Of course, after a while, all that crying made women want to gag, and what followed was the inevitable backlash against male crying.

Look what happened to Alan Alda's career. One minute he's misty-eyed over operating room sexism on "M*A*S*H," the next minute he's working a Knights of Columbus convention in Des Moines.

Today, male crying is clearly acceptable, but it's not as, um celebrated as it once was.

But try telling that to my old friend Monte. Monte's last crying jag came in a packed stadium while a group of us watched a football game in the rain. Suddenly, the sun peeked through the clouds and a rainbow appeared.

Of course, the rest of us recognized this as big trouble, because it meant that Monte would soon go to pieces and embarrass us.

Sure enough, as he gazed at the sky, his shoulders began to shake and pretty soon tears streamed down his face.

"It's so... so *beautiful!*" he sobbed.

Finally, somebody reached over and smacked him with a half-empty can of Budweiser and told him to knock it off. Which was only right. Here we were, surrounded by 60,000 screaming drunks who wanted to split the opposing quarterback's head like a cantaloupe, and Monte was being *moved* by a rainbow.

Heck, there were three or four women sitting behind us who wanted to take a poke at the little jerk themselves.

As a general rule of thumb, fallen preachers, such as Jim Bakker and Jimmy Swaggart, are terrific criers, men who can summon wonderfully deep, mournful sobs that seem to emanate from some dark place within their souls.

Watching Jim Bakker blubbering and carrying on before they dragged him off to the slammer, I thought: Now *that's* crying!

Let me hasten to add that if they were dragging *me* off to spend the next seven to ten years in a dank prison cell shared with an oddly affectionate weight-lifter named Todd, I would be crying too — as well as screaming and hanging onto someone's pants leg. Oh, you talk about a scene. You'd need five beefy U.S. marshals with crowbars to pry my hands loose.

Unfortunately, though, some men give crying a bad name. Because instead of letting forth at the appropriate time with a river of tears, they sort of... *sniffle*.

Look, if you're going to cry, cry like a man! Don't cry like some three-year-old who just took a tumble on his Big Wheel.

Of course, in the pantheon of modern-day crybabies, one man stands alone. Ladies and gentlemen, put your hands together for a major star, a super talent, Mr. Jerry Lewis!

You want a river of tears? Then check out Jerry's Labor Day telethon for Muscular Dystrophy. Great cause, sure. But when the show finally grinds to a close, and the tote board number goes over last year's pledge total, there's Jerry: shirt collar open, tuxedo bow tie askew, slick hair plastered with sweat against his forehead, hugging Ed McMahon and sobbing like someone just ran over his dog.

Say what you will about Jerry Lewis. But the man can flat-out *weep*.

So could Sammy Davis, Jr., may he rest in peace. Sammy would take the stage during Jerry's telethon and start rapping about some "super-talented cat I know in L.A., I mean, I love this cat, and now the man is going through some hard times..." And next thing you know, Sammy's voice would catch, he'd become a quivering wreck, and some stage hand would have to walk him back to the dressing room.

Sammy set the crying standard for us all.

No restroom for the weary

If you are anywhere near as vigilant as I am — and frankly, that's probably not possible — you've noticed an alarming trend in public restrooms.

In the old days, it was easy to figure out which restroom you were supposed to use.

A man would use the restrooms identified by a sign saying "Men" or "Gentlemen." A woman would use the restrooms identified as being for "Women" or "Ladies."

Life was good. The system worked beautifully. And as befitted our status as the greatest nation on Earth, no citizen had to pause outside a restroom, scratch his or her head thoughtfully, and say: "Gee, I... I wonder which door would best suit my personal hygiene needs?"

Then, I don't know, something happened. Me, I blame it on the '70s. In addition to giving us disco, lime-green leisure suits and long sideburns, the '70s ushered in the era of the cute, gimmicky restroom sign.

Pretty soon restrooms had signs that said "Guys" and "Dolls." Or the supremely irritating "Stags" and "Does."

It was enough to make you sick. Not to mention confused. Bars and restaurants were the worst offenders, especially "theme" bars and restaurants.

Country and western bars had restrooms for "Buckaroos" and "Buckarettes." Seafood joints marked their restrooms with "Buoys" and "Gulls" — that was perhaps the all-time worst.

If ever there was a time to leave the country, this was it. And they wondered why I kept my passport up-to-date.

(*True story*: I once ate in a famous New York restaurant designed like the inside of a train. The seats looked like they were pulled from Amtrak club cars, the menus read like train schedules, the waiters were dressed as conductors, etc. You get the picture. A slice of hell on Earth.

(Anyway, fearing the worst, I excused myself at one point and asked the maitre d': "Where's the little engineer's room?"

("Sir," he replied stiffly, "do you mean the *men's room?*"

(Naturally, I was mortified. But only for about two seconds.

("It's back in the caboose," he answered.)

That brings us to the latest disturbing new trend in restroom marking: Stick figures.

I first noticed this nightmarish development when I visited the office building where a friend worked.

The place was one of those cold imposing, steel-and-glass corporate centers devoted solely to the making of money, which meant I felt right at home. In fact, I had to check the urge to distribute my resume right then and there.

Anyway, during a fun discussion with my friend about mergers, acquisitions and the best way to foreclose on an elderly widow's house, I had to use the restroom. One of the office androids with the requisite pinstriped suit and vacant personality pointed me in the right direction.

But when I got to the restrooms, I was faced with this dilemma: Which door to enter? Neither door had a sign saying "Men" or "Women." Instead, each had a tiny stick figure affixed to it.

Now, here is the thing about stick figures: By and large, they are sexually ambiguous. Call me dense, but I usually can't tell a boy stick figure from a girl stick figure.

Then I noticed that one stick figure had a lower torso, and it was in the shape of an inverted V. Was that a woman stick figure in a skirt? Or a man stick figure wearing a raincoat?

Anyway, you can only dwell on this kind of stuff for so long when nature calls. So, finally, I just picked a door and walked in. Spotting the urinals, I knew I was OK.

Since then, I've noticed that stick figures are now identifying restrooms in shopping malls.

And the reaction of the people who use these restrooms is always the same. They have to pause for a moment to make sure they're going in the right door.

You should not have to pause and think on your way to the restroom, especially in an airport. Airports are nerve-wracking places to begin with. People hurry about wrapped up in their own thoughts, which usually center around their plane slamming into the side of a cliff or setting down for an emergency landing in some desolate Iowa cornfield.

The last thing a person in an airport needs is the added stress that comes with having to decipher stick figures on a restroom door.

Although I suppose *anything* is better than "Buoys and Gulls."

Letters dress up *SI* swimsuit issue

I have before me the notorious swimsuit issue of *Sports Illustrated*, the one about which there's always so much fuss.

This is my favorite issue of *SI*, though it's not just because I like to keep up with the latest styles in beachwear. And it's not just because the models have extensive athletic backgrounds ("Kim was a competitive swimmer in high school... Renee plays tennis and swims"), which is no doubt why they were selected.

No, the swimsuit issue is my favorite because it means all those letters from outraged subscribers will appear in the next issue of *SI*.

You know the letters I'm talking about.

"Dear Editor:

"My husband and I are simple Amish farmers. Our 13-year-old son Jedediah aspired to be a simple Amish farmer, too. But ever since your filthy swimsuit issue arrived in the mail, he refuses to get behind the plow.

"Now all he does is sit up in his room and smoke pot and watch porno movies.

"P.S. This never happened with Field and Stream. Cancel my subscription."

Or:

"Dear Editor:

"As a high school basketball coach here in Clarksville, Miss., I was appalled at the disgusting photographs of semi-naked women that appeared in your swimsuit issue. I caught Billy Joe, our leading scorer, passing the magazine around before our recent game against Leesburg.

"We lost 101-50. Billy Joe went 2-for-22 from the floor. Cancel my subscription immediately.

"P.S. This Renee —does she have a jump shot? Billy Joe ran off with the stripper down at Earl's Sunset Lounge."

Anyway, back to this week's swimsuit issue.

The setting for the issue is the sunny clime of the Dominican Republic. Real sports fans recognize the Dominican Republic as the homeland of superstar dictator Rafael Trujillo, whose favorite sport was having his enemies thrown to the sharks.

On the cover is model Elle Macpherson. In a publisher's note, *SI* advises that Elle is just another humble ex-jock. ("Macpherson... was a backstroker who competed from a very early age at home in Australia.")

Here, however, Elle is wearing a skimpy green number. The same skimpy green number would get *you* thrown out of any swim-meet you tried to enter. It would also probably get you arrested — or at the very least a job as a Vegas show girl.

The skimpy green number is called a tank suit. It is designed by H2O. It lists for $72.

I hope that's not too technical. It's just that the swimsuit issue tends to lapse into that kind of arcane jock jargon.

Anyway, turning to Page 3, we find a shot of model Kim Alexis.

Kim, we are told, is a marathoner. She's shown in this photo jogging in a racy suit (Mistral, $44). Curiously, she is shown jogging on an active airport runway.

You can tell it's an active runway because a twin-propeller plane can be seen taking off directly over Kim's right shoulder.

OK, fine. Let's say Kim really *is* a serious marathoner. I'm here to tell her, if one of those prop planes smacks her, her split times are going to suffer dramatically.

Turning to Page 98 and the main, er, body of the story, we are greeted by 34 pages of swimsuit photos.

Again, in keeping with the athletic flavor of the issue, the models are shown engaging in various sports.

Kathy is shown lounging on a golf course in a bikini (*Giorgio di Sant'Angelo*, $75).

Kim is shown checking out her scuba gear in a latex suit (*Liza Bruce*, $120).

Carol is shown leaning against a rock in something red and black (*Darling Rio*, $45).

Kim is shown sunning herself on a beach. With her eyes closed. In a tank suit (*Adrienne Vittadini*, $56).

Anyway, you get the idea. Just a bunch of wholesome jocks frolicking in their swimsuits. And working on their games. At least that's the way I see it.

And that's why I decided to fire off my own letter to *SI*:

"*Dear Editor:*

"*Just finished browsing through your swimsuit issue. The athletes this year were swell looking, as they are every year. And there were some neat new styles that really caught my eye, especially that red-and-black number Carol wears for rock-leaning.*

"*Enclosed please find a check for double the amount of a regular subscription. Keep the change. You guys deserve it.*

"*P.S. I never did this with Field and Stream.*"

Baseball's just a game (not)

With baseball having entered its post-season phase, the cliches are flying around major league clubhouses like too many wads of balled-up tape.

What follows is a comprehensive interpretation of baseball-speak:

"We're taking it one game at a time."

(Our team has no shot to win. N-O-N-E. This time next week, I'll be packing a 9 mm and heading for two weeks of golf in Florida.)

"We have a lot of respect for their pitching."

(Their ace is a violent sociopath. He's beaned three of our players.)

"Their bullpen closer has a real live arm."

(And possibly cataracts. Half his pitches wind up in the stands.)

"Their batting order scares you from top to bottom."

(All nine guys in the regular lineup have been brought up on weapons charges.)

"The fans, the media, nobody thought we'd get this far."

(Frankly, half our team has been in rehab.)

"We never stopped believing in ourselves."

(Our 12-step program is the best around.)

"Everyone on this club gives you 110 percent."

(Our trainer hands out greenies like they're Skittles.)

"Look at a guy like Johnson, all the work he did in the off-season, the tremendous improvement he's made."

(Johnson's on steroids.)

"And Malone bats .320 with 36 homers — look how well he rebounded from last season."

(Malone's in the last year of a long-term contract. Once he signs a new one, he won't hit his weight.)

"All year long, this team has battled back from adversity."

(Yep, our top slugger got loaded and rammed his Porsche into a bridge. Our bullpen closer was arrested for beating his wife. And our shortstop was seen at a nightclub in a cocktail dress and high heels.)

"We've had *our* share of injuries, too."

(Our catcher slammed his hand through a window during a bout of amphetamine psychosis.)

"We've got a real blue-collar team."

(Our players aren't afraid to scratch themselves in public.)

"We've got a lunch-pail work ethic."

(At house parties, our players have been known to spit on the carpet.)

"We've got one heckuva close team."

(Some of us have swapped girlfriends.)

"It might be the closest team I've ever been on."

(We've even swapped wives.)

"This is it. There's no tomorrow."

(Then again, I make $4 million a year, live in a mansion, drive a Ferrari Testarosa, and date a former Playmate of the Year. I'll probably be able to drag myself out of bed the day after we lose.)

"No question about it —our backs are against the wall."

(The only way we'll win is if the other team's plane goes down.)

"We're just not swinging the bat well."

(Our manager has ordered new drug tests.)

"My home run today? Well, I wasn't thinking home run in that situation. I was just trying to drive the ball."

(Check the instant replay. I probably had my eyes closed.)

"Pressure? There's no pressure on us to win."

(If we lose this series, they'll be hunting us down with dogs.)

"Besides, pressure's what you put on yourself."

(Tie score, bottom of the ninth... please God, don't let them hit it to me!)

"This time of year, it's not about money. It's about pride."

(It's about money.)

"After all, how often do you get a shot at the World Series?"

(It's about money.)

"Winning the MVP trophy would be nice, but I'm not concerned about individual awards. I'm interested in just one thing — winning."

(I'd kill to win the MVP. My agent says it's worth an extra $2 million in my next contract.)

"It's gonna be tough to win three in a row playing at their place."

(We're doomed. Do yourself a favor. Call your bookmaker. Unload on the other team.)

"They have some of the league's most spirited fans."

(Every night is like Nickel Beer Night in Tijuana.)

"And they're some of the most knowledgeable fans around."
(Some nuts in the right field stands figured out a way to shoot nails at me with a slingshot.)
"But our feeling is: It ain't over 'til it's over."
(It's over.)
"It ain't over 'til the fat lady sings."
(Here she comes! Good Lord, look at the size of her!)

Raised by Wolves

It's a good life, kidding around

As I wrestled the two-year-old into his pajamas and he threw a crisp violent uppercut at my head to show his appreciation, it occurred to me what a wonderful life the boy leads.

Let's face it, there's basically no pressure on you when you're two.

You ease into the day with a little "Barney the dinosaur" on TV. Then it's on to "Sesame Street" to see what's happening with Bert and Ernie, and then — where does the time go? — someone's serving you breakfast.

After that, you color for a while, or take the Big Wheel for a spin, or play with your toy trucks. Then it's time for lunch. And after that — this is the part that's truly amazing — they ask if you're ready for a *nap!*

In fact, they actually *carry* you to your room and tuck you in. Then, if anybody makes any noise, everyone else in the house goes "Shhh!" as if the pope were sleeping in the next bedroom.

(If you're an adult, just *try* taking a nap. Even before you drift off, someone will be poking you in the back with a broom handle and telling you to get off your duff and go rake the leaves.)

When you're two, you get to eat what you want, too. If you don't like the green beans on your plate, hey, don't eat 'em! You might even fling your plate on the floor. What are your parents gonna do? Send you to your room? Yell at you? Let's face it, at age two, you're basically immune to criticism.

When you're two, you get to wear the coolest clothes, too, all sorts of neat T-shirts and overalls, and no one calls you a hayseed or greaser.

It's hard to believe, but people actually compliment you on your *underwear!* Your mom will be dressing you and your dad will peek his head in the room and say: "Hey, what do you have on there, partner? Thomas the Train undies. Boy, they're cool!"

It makes you feel like a million bucks. And it's the same with pajamas. All you have to do is come downstairs at bedtime in a snazzy pair of Barbie jammies and people will make such a big fuss you'd think Hillary Clinton just walked into the room.

When you're two, you have absolutely no financial problems, either. You don't even have to carry money.

When you and your family go to McDonald's, no one expects you to reach in your pocket and say: "Here, lemme get the Big Macs..."

Or when your parents pull their car up to the gas pump, no one's waiting for you to whip out your Sunoco credit card and say: "Dad, I got the gas. No, c'mon, you bought last time."

In fact, even though you never offer to pay for a single thing, people will *insist* on buying you things.

If you're in the drugstore staring longingly at the M&M's, the odds are good that one of your parents will notice and buy the M&M's for you.

Here you didn't say a word and you end up with a 55-cent package of candy. I don't see how you can beat that!

Another neat thing about being two: You're guaranteed your very own seat in the car.

Everybody else in the family has to scramble for a seat. Your brothers and sisters are always elbowing each other and whining: "I got the front seat!"

But you never have to sink to that level. You can remain nice and calm. Because you *know* where *you're* sitting.

When you're two, people are impressed by the most innocuous things you do.

Try this little experiment: Grab a crayon, scribble a few lines on a piece of paper, and hand it to your parents. Now watch them ooh and aah about what a great picture you drew.

Anyone with any brains can see it's junk. But your parents will go nuts over it anyway.

Nine times out of ten, they'll even put your, ahem, *artwork* on the refrigerator with one of those little pineapple magnets.

You'll be sitting there shaking your head and thinking, "Geez, it's just a bunch of squiggly *lines*," but your parents will be carrying on like it's a Monet or something.

It's the same thing when you put your shoes on by yourself. Let's face it: There's nothing to putting on a pair of shoes, even at age two. You open the Velcro tabs, stick your feet in, and pull the tabs over. No big deal, right?

Right. But do it in front of your parents and they'll practically turn cartwheels in your presence. They might even buy you an ice cream! Just for putting on your *shoes!*

And for the rest of the day they'll be talking about you like you're another Jonas Salk.

It doesn't take much to make some people happy, that's for sure.

Preschool holds the secrets of life

From my new bestseller *All I Really Need to Know I Learned Even Before Kindergarten, In Preschool, I Think It Was*:

• You know those plastic things in the wall? The, um, electrical outlets? Don't stick your fingers in them. It can really hurt.

• Sharing is all well and good. But if you split a doughnut, you'd be foolish not to keep the bigger half. Especially if it has more jelly.

• If someone hits you, start screaming and drop to the floor. When that person bends over and asks, "Are you all right?" you'll have a clear shot at kicking him in the groin.

• People are more inclined to believe you if you end a statement with the words "swear to God."

• If you pull the cat's tail when others are around, he'll tell on you and you'll get in trouble. It's better to wait until everyone else is asleep.

• Don't take things that aren't yours. Unless it's a towel that says "Holiday Inn" or something.

• When people tell you it "tastes like chicken," it probably tastes like a bucket of warm spit.

• I am me. And you are you. So there's no way I could be you. Or you me. Outside of something really spooky happening.

• If you're trying to work, and the person next to you is being noisy, lean over and say: "Ex-cuse me, but I have a good mind to whack you upside the head with a ruler." Then do it.

• There's nothing wrong with peanut butter and jelly sandwiches. But if you have them day after day after day... I'd at least try a cheese-steak sub once in a while.

• If you see an automobile bearing down on you at a busy intersection, get off the street fast.

• Take credit for the good things, and blame others when things go wrong.

• Always ask someone to taste the soup first. If that person shrieks "YEOWW!" and starts fanning his mouth, it's probably too hot to eat.

• If someone is being mean to you, quietly say to that person: "My dad works for the Gambino Family."

• Short of finding a footlocker crammed with $200,000 in small, unmarked bills, a chocolate chip cookie is about as good as it gets.

• If you are very fat, it would not hurt to mix in a salad occasionally.

• It's not that your mother was lying but... I myself have run carrying scissors many times and never poked anyone's eye out with them.

• White people, black people, red people, yellow people — we're all the same inside. Except for Cher.

• A nap really helps. I take one for eight hours each night and feel much better upon awakening.

• Bananas are so superior to apples it's not even funny.

• Don't say bad things about another person, especially if that person's attorney is present.

• When you go out in the world, remember two things: Mastercard and Visa.

• If you lose something, don't waste your time trying to find it. Ask your mom to find it.

• Big hand on the 12, little hand on the 6, it's time for dinner.

• You will hurt your fingers badly by poking them in a fan, even if it's set on "low."

• Live a balanced life — learn and think and paint and draw and sing and dance. But keep it to yourself, or people will think you're some kind of obsessive, over-achieving wacko.

• If anyone were to actually attempt the maneuvers described in the song "This Old Man," that person would be placed in a locked ward.

• The best way to get out of trouble is to say: "I didn't do it. She did."

• When someone gives you something, thank them. But make it clear you expected something else, *too*.

• People with really good jobs rarely move their lips when reading.

• Always play fair. With your luck, there'll be a surveillance camera around.

• Hold hands when you leave the house. But let the other person know that if something bad happens, he's on his own.

• It sounds like a glamorous profession, but there are very few cowboys around anymore.

• If you want something badly enough, it can be yours ... except for Cindy Crawford.

• Love is not something you can hold, but it *is* something you can buy.

• Clean up your own mess, unless, of course, you're only renting.

The natural childbirth scam

This seems as good a time as any to rail anew against the most massive fraud ever perpetrated on the American public: the concept of natural childbirth.

With the birth of our third child expected in May, my wife and I are often approached by well-meaning but dim-witted individuals who, desperately fighting through the fog that's enveloped their brains, note that my wife's stomach has ballooned to the size of Desert Storm commander Gen. Norman Schwarzkopf's.

Then these individuals arch an eyebrow and ask in that syrupy, Earth Mother voice, whether we'll be attending refresher childbirth classes.

Nine times out of ten, a two-by-four isn't lying around so you can whack these people across the forehead.

So, suppressing our irritation, we explain that no, if it's all right with you, Mr. or Ms. Busybody, we *won't* be attending refresher childbirth classes.

And the reason we *won't* is that this would be sort of like attending refresher classes in "Time: How to Waste It in Idleness and Sloth."

The idea that deep-breathing exercises, instruction films of the "Our Friend the Cervix" variety and spirited discussions of the uterus will help when an eight pound child begins inching down a narrow birth canal is, of course, preposterous.

So when the big day arrives and my wife goes into labor, we will calmly drive to the hospital. We will calmly wait out the initial contractions, as we did during the births of our first two children: she'll be moaning and angrily throwing cups of shaved ice when I (politely) ask her to keep the noise down so I can hear the TV.

And when the labor pains finally intensify, why, we will calmly drop to our knees and beg our obstetrician for massive quantities of drugs.

Whether my wife takes them or not is her business: Me, I'll be wolfing down everything I can get my hands on.

I expect some good stuff, too: Morphine, ether, Johnny Walker Black. (Worse comes to worse, I'll settle for someone knocking me out with a croquet mallet.)

Ironically, childbirth classes continue to ensnare wave after wave of unsuspecting parents-to-be, even though natural childbirth has been largely discredited (it seems to me) as a propaganda tool of touchy-feely ex-hippies, leftists and New Age prophets.

The classes themselves begin on an eerie note, with the arrival of any number of tense, unsmiling couples lugging — of all things — pillows under their arms.

Impromptu pajama party? Tragic outbreak of narcolepsy? Bizarre satanic ritual wherein one chanting partner smothers the other as an old Doors album wails in the background?

Who knows? First the couples must endure a dreary orientation speech/pep talk, delivered by some wild-eyed birthing instructor (usually named "Susie" for reasons that are not exactly clear).

In the breathless, chirpy tones of a career Moonie, Susie, in a disjointed 20-minute address, will attempt to convince the couples that:

1. Natural childbirth — which has been likened to having one's pelvic region pulled apart by teams of sturdy oxen — is the greatest experience of a woman's life.

2. Inhaling and exhaling properly can largely replace powerful narcotics in masking the pain of childbirth.

3. The male partner is every bit as important to the birthing process as the female, and should put the sports section down long enough to offer emotional support and serve as "breathing coach."

Well. Dazed and reeling from this subversive gibberish, the couples must then sit through a series of grainy, full-color movies of a baby being born that generally rival the Battle of Gettysburg for blood-flow content.

Often pictures or plastic models of a woman's reproductive system are passed around the room and examined with an air of clinical detachment, as if they were sale items at a Tupperware party.

By now, even the most gung-ho, "no-drugs-for-us" couples are generally in a state of intense emotional upheaval. With the adrenalin surging and their bodies in full "fight-or-flight" response, many will flee the room in terror. Some will actually hurl themselves through the plasterboard walls, leaving a cartoon-like silhouette and smoke trails in their wake.

Those too numb to make a run for it are doomed to a pointless series of deep-breathing exercises, with Susie dashing about the room like a fox terrier on Methedrine squeaking: "Peggy and Ralph, you're doing great!"

God help us all.

Real men don't wear pajamas

The way I look at it, real men don't wear pajamas to bed.

Real men wear underwear. If they wear anything else to bed, it's a Pittsburgh Steelers T-shirt. And a smile. This is considered by many to be the official hip sleepwear of the American male.

The point is, you just can't look hip in pajamas.

A man in pajamas automatically looks like Ward Cleaver stumbling onto a two a.m. bull session between Wally and the Beaver.

It seems to me that the only people who look cool in pajamas are kids.

A kid slips on a nifty pair of Flintstones jammies or a smart-looking Mickey Mouse number and, let's face it, he looks like a million bucks.

Whereas no matter the cut or quality of a man's pajamas, he still looks like Dagwood Bumstead letting the dog out in the middle of the night.

Besides, there's a basic question of taste to be addressed here. After a hard day of dodgeball, video games, riding bikes, etc., you don't want your six-year-old hitting the sack in his underwear.

It just doesn't look right. This isn't an Army barracks he's living in. Let a six-year-old sleep in underwear and the next thing you know, the kid will be firing up a Marlboro and downing a steaming cup of java.

No, the rule of thumb is this: Once you're old enough to shave, you're old enough to ditch those silly Bugs Bunny jammies.

It's basically the same thing with bathrobes. A man puts on a bathrobe and instantly looks like Ricky Ricardo killing time before a gig at the Copacabana.

Oh, sure, in his own way Ricky was cool. He had that slicked-back hair and that syrupy Cuban accent that drove all the women crazy.

Plus, he had a pretty neat job as a band leader, apparently pulling down some big bucks, judging by the way Fred and Ethel Mertz talked.

So, yeah, Ricky Ricardo was cool.

But here's the thing: *He was cool in 1957.*

The man comes back today with that pompadour and that hyper "Ay, caramba!" nonsense, he's just another nerdy, middle-aged guy from Havana.

And, if he's wearing that goofy bathrobe, the only gig he'll work is in the locked unit at the state hospital.

There's another downside to a man wearing a bathrobe, which I bring up only because it might save someone's life.

Let's say you're awakened in the middle of the night by a loud noise in the basement. And your wife and kids, as usual, are too chicken to check it out.

So it's up to you to go down there and confront the psychotic burglar who surely awaits in the darkness with a chainsaw.

Anyway, you get out of bed and quietly slip on your bathrobe. Big mistake there, Mister. In fact, you probably just signed your own death warrant.

Think you're going to frighten this psycho burglar off if you come padding downstairs in a silk bathrobe?

Are you kidding? He'll think it's Sebastian Cabot about to fix himself a warm glass of milk.

And he'll just go back to doing whatever it was he was doing, which was probably oiling his chainsaw and disconnecting your Sony Trinitron.

Even if you come downstairs brandishing a baseball bat, you just can't look menacing in a bathrobe.

Believe me, the only way you'll scare this guy off is if he starts laughing so hard he can't breathe.

Or if he thinks it's Peter Sellers come back to life and runs shrieking out the door.

Now, if you confront the psycho burglar in your underwear and a Steelers T-shirt, the man HAS to give you some respect.

Don't get me wrong. Somewhere, in the midst of the psychotic haze that envelops him, he's thinking: "Nice T-shirt." But he still might fire up the chainsaw and turn you into hamburger.

While we're on this subject, let's clear up one more thing about male sleeping attire: Real men don't sleep naked, either.

Sure, if you're a bachelor and so many women come to your apartment that it looks like a Jazzercise class, you might spend the night sans underwear and Steelers T-shirt.

But once you're a family man, you have to cut that out. You can't have kids wandering into your bedroom and thinking: "Whoa! Must be shooting the new Richard Gere film here!"

Even the coolest guy in history, James Bond, retained some sense of modesty in his sleepwear.

Remember how the bad guys were always sneaking into his bedroom to shoot him, pour acid on his face, or drop tarantulas on his chest?

Each time Bond wised up, threw off the covers, and kicked some tail, he was wearing *something*: boxer shorts, swim trunks, etc.

Even if some hot-looking babe like Ursula Andress was catching some Z's next to him, 007 was cool enough to cover up.

And not with some silly-looking sailboat jammies, either.

An earring beats a spike

If memory serves, I had just drifted off for a nap, maybe even entered the REM phase, when the 11-year-old asked if we could talk about the "earring thing" again.

According to him, earrings are cool and all his friends wear earrings, not to mention just about every guy in his school, and he'd like to wear one, too, except his old man is a fascist geek.

He didn't actually use the term "fascist geek," but that's certainly what he was thinking.

"Look," I said, "if your mother and I let you wear an earring, you'll want a tattoo next, something with a big skull and flying dragons, and then you'll join an outlaw motorcycle gang and take up with a wild woman named Louise who'll talk you into holding up a convenience store at three in the morning, for which you'll get caught and do hard time while Louise takes up with your best friend Elmo.

"*That's* what an earring can lead to. You ask me, it's just not worth it."

He walked away shaking his head, and I sure couldn't blame him. It sounded like a lot of crap to me, too, but it was the best crap I could come up with on the spur of the moment.

That's the thing about kids: They're always asking you for something without giving you time to make up a good story. After a while it really gets annoying.

Actually, I don't have a problem with my son wearing an earring, if that's what he wants to do when he's a little older.

The fact is, I wanted an earring myself when I was young, except I ran into a little problem, the problem being that I was too chicken. This condition came as the result of the time me and Jim Cusimano decided to get our ears pierced.

We ended up in this head shop — look, this was back in 1970 and everyone was terminally stupid — where a man with long, stringy hair and maybe three teeth gave us each an ice cube to numb our ear lobes. Jim volunteered to go first, which was fine with me. In fact, I may have even pushed him into the chair ahead of me.

Then the man pulled out a needle the size of a harpoon and jabbed Jim in the ear lobe. Jim, the toughest linebacker on the football team, did not handle this well, screaming and carrying on.

"Well, forget *this*," I thought. "Maybe a nice paisley shirt would be the way to go here." So I never got my ear pierced and neither did Jim, for that matter — he freaked out so much the man gave us our money back and told us to get out.

The point is, I am certainly not anti-earring, although I favor tasteful studs or small hoops for men, not those big, dangly things that look like something Lola Falana wears on stage at the Sahara.

If you're a guy and you show up for work on the loading dock with an earring like that, people are gonna talk.

Still, compared to some things kids are wearing these days, a guy with an earring is no big deal anymore.

Are you kidding? If you're a parent, your kid might come to you and say: "I'm thinking of getting a nose ring, maybe something with five holes. Unless you think that's too *busy*."

Or he could suddenly show up at the breakfast table with a nipple ring. Or, I don't know, a six-inch silver spike implanted through his cheek.

So an earring is no big deal. Hell, whenever my kid asks me for an earring, I'm tempted to reach in my pocket and say: "Look, here's a few bucks — get yourself a *couple* of earrings. See if any of your friends want earrings, too. But, hey — no spikes through the cheek, OK?"

Most guys with earrings look pretty good, with one obvious exception: old guys. I remember when Ed Bradley of "60 Minutes" wore an earring. It just didn't look right, like Ed was trying just a *little* too hard to be hip.

He'd be interviewing someone like Yasser Arafat, and you could see Arafat was thinking: "What's with the old dude and the earring? Wait'll I tell the boys back in Tunis about this."

Of course, times have changed and now Ed Bradley could probably interview the pope on network television with a spike through his cheek. Especially if it was a small, tasteful spike.

Wiffleball is not for sissies

As every clear-thinking American knows, wiffleball remains our greatest backyard game, better than badminton or horseshoes or any other sissy sport where you don't even bleed.

Wiffleball is for anyone willing to shrug off a full-speed collision with the tool shed and six months of subsequent blackouts just to snare a grounder up the middle.

Look, if you're one of these crybabies who runs into a hammock tracking a fly ball, gets yoked off his feet, and then whines about spending three weeks in a neck brace, sorry, perhaps croquet is more your speed.

But if you're *not* afraid of being wheeled into an operating room occasionally — and let's face it, that's what they have anesthesia for — maybe you have what it takes to play this game.

Really, if you think about it, no other backyard game demands such a range of athleticism and dark, suicidal urges.

Shuffleboard? Please. My eyes are starting to close. Frisbee? They should have buried that sport during the Age of Aquarius. Lawn darts? That's it. I'm officially asleep.

The beauty of wiffleball is that it's a sport the whole family can enjoy — *or* it can lead to endless bickering and bruised feelings, as is more commonly the case.

Certainly, a sullen pall seemed to hang in the air during our first family wiffleball game of this season.

The day dawned sunny and cool, perfect for that harrowing ride to the hospital should someone snap an ankle in one of the many holes the dog had dug.

In the interest of saving time, I quickly chose up sides. The key here, of course, is to stack the team in your favor.

What you try to do is choose a lot of young, athletic people for your squad.

Ex-college ballplayers, Green Berets, women helicopter pilots, varsity softball champions, combat nurses — these are the folks you want in *your* line-up.

On the other team you stick all the pencil-necked computer geeks, pasty-faced math teachers, guys who throw like girls, asthmatics, drunks, people with heart conditions, the wheelchair-bound, narcoleptics, pregnant women, even babies.

Then you ask in a loud voice: "OK, are these fair teams?"

Before anyone has a chance to respond, you run up to home plate, grab a bat and shout: "All right, we're up first!"

Once again, this strategy worked to perfection this year, as the teams ended up being me, my 10-year-old son and our 14-year-old neighbor against my wife, our 7-year-old daughter and 23-month-old son.

Naturally, my wife started whining that the teams "weren't fair," even when we pointed out the obvious advantages of having a toddler on your team.

I mean, the kid has a strike zone of what, *six inches*? How do you pitch to someone like that? If the kid had any brains, he'd keep the bat on his shoulder and draw a walk every time.

But this kid... I don't know, you can't *talk* to him. Instead of crouching down like Ricky Henderson and making it impossible to be pitched to, he's swinging from his heels on every pitch.

I felt kind of sorry for him — but not sorry enough to ease up on him during his first at-bat. So I fed him three fastballs — WHAM! WHAM! WHAM! — and he struck out swinging. Didn't take it real well, either. Started acting like a two-year-old, if you want to know the truth.

Things did not improve a great deal when my daughter came up to bat next.

"Remember, she's only seven!" my wife shouted.

"She's got a bat in her hands, doesn't she?!" I snarled.

I mean, what was I supposed to do here? Let her take me deep just 'cause she's seven? How's it going to sound when word gets around the neighborhood that little kids are rocking me for extra bases?

So I started her off with two fastballs — WHAM! WHAM! — that (with all due modesty) were nothing but a blur. Then I threw her a curve that broke somewhere out by the tire swing.

She waved at it feebly for strike three and walked dejectedly away.

"Now she's all upset!" my wife said.

Look, my thinking here is this: She's young, she'll get over it. Fifteen years from now, I don't see her sitting on a Scandinavian leather chair in some analyst's office, sobbing into a Kleenex that her life is all screwed up because daddy once K'd her on an 0-2 fastball.

Anyway, along about the third inning, trailing 28-3, the other team walked off the field — just like they do *every* year.

Then my wife, who's the biggest crybaby of them all, accused me of running up the score and not playing fair and blah, blah, blah.

It's a wonderful game, wiffleball.

Although certain people take it a bit too seriously for my taste.

Other Reasons to Go on Living

Take charge, if that's OK

I recently attended a self-assertiveness workshop called "Taking Charge of Your Life," which I really didn't want to go to, but my wife talked me into it.

Fifteen of us met in a classroom at a local community college. The room was very hot and I wanted to open a window.

But then I thought: What if the others don't want the window open? What if they look at me funny? What if I open the window and someone walks over and slams it shut and glares at me?

Suddenly a small, balding man with stooped shoulders entered the room and slammed his briefcase on the desk. Scowling, he said his name was Richard, and that he was our instructor.

"Let's get one thing straight," he said. "Don't *anyone* call me Dick. Anyone calls me Dick, I will slap that person silly."

As the first order of business, Richard passed out little cards and had us write down what we hoped to get out of the class.

I wrote down my goals and added: "Room is very hot. Could we open a window, please?"

Then I underlined the word "please" three times, so Richard would know I meant business.

He read each card silently and shot a withering look in my direction but made no attempt to open a window.

A woman named Mary was the first to speak. Mary said she was having a problem getting through to her husband. She'd come home from work and start telling him about her day, and, without a word, her husband would turn on ESPN and start watching a bass fishing tournament. It was very disconcerting to her.

The other night she was sitting at the kitchen table and reading aloud from a letter her mother had sent them, only to discover that her husband had slipped out of the house and gone to the gym.

"Swat him over the head with a newspaper," Richard said.

"Beg your pardon?" Mary said.

"Crack 'im right here," Richard said, pointing to an area near his temple. "He'll start paying attention."

Mary said she wasn't sure she could do that, due to her Methodist upbringing and a general tendency toward non-violence.

"People like you make me want to *puke!*" Richard said.

I looked at Mary. She was twisting her Kleenex with both hands now and her lower lip was trembling badly.

A man named Chester spoke next. He said he was a bus mechanic and worked with a fellow who insisted on ending every sentence with the word 'kay?

God, it was irritating! All day long, the man would say, "Hand me that wrench over there, 'kay?" and "Almost time for lunch, 'kay?" and "Let's grab a beer after work, 'kay?"

It was driving Chester nuts. He wanted to tell the fellow how annoying this practice was, but had yet to summon the nerve.

Richard said the solution was simple: "Grab him by the collar and tell him to knock it off, or you'll kick the stuffing out of him."

A moon-faced young man named Mario then began detailing a three-year relationship with a thoroughly overbearing girlfriend, a woman from Boston who insisted on making every decision for the couple.

Jason — we later found out he was an elementary school teacher — loudly announced that Mario sure sounded like a wuss.

"Who you calling a wuss?" said Mario, his jaw tightening.

I had made up my mind to open a window when suddenly Mario walked over to Jason and decked him with a punch.

Jason got up right away and started swinging, even through he was crying. The two went at it pretty good until Richard and a couple of guys broke it up.

Now Mary was sobbing: "He never listens... doesn't care if I live or die, really..."

I was finding it hard to concentrate.

Then Chester keeled over in his chair. It was probably the heat. One minute he looked fine; the next minute his head slammed against the desk and he was out cold.

The class broke up ten minutes later when the ambulance arrived.

Two policemen showed up, too. Apparently someone had heard all the screaming and dialed 911.

I gave my statement to the cops and went home. There, everyone asked: "So, how was the class?"

"Oh," I said, "about what you'd expect."

The airheads of the airwaves

One morning on talk radio:

HOST: "...and the CIA parachutes in a couple of midget agents masquerading as Iraqi children. Then one of 'em ices Saddam when he visits their school. Anyway, that's my plan. What do *you* think? 555-WHEW is the number here on the Marty Behan Show. Let's go to Larry in northwest Baltimore."

CALLER: "Marty, remember the old Road Runner cartoons?"

HOST: "Absolutely."

CALLER: "Remember how Wile E. Coyote strapped himself to an ACME rocket to catch the Road Runner?"

HOST: "What's your point?"

CALLER: "We get some Green Berets, strap each one to a rocket and launch 'em into Baghdad to get Saddam."

HOST: "I have no problem with that. Rod from Towson, you're on the air."

CALLER: "Marty, the coyote also launched himself once from a giant ACME super-stretch slingshot embedded in the desert floor."

HOST: "So?"

CALLER: "We set up a slingshot somewhere in Saudi Arabia and shoot a couple of Navy SEALS onto the roof of Saddam's palace. End of problem."

HOST: "Betty from Catonsville."

CALLER: "Marty, did I hear you say earlier that Hillary Clinton engages in satanic rituals?"

HOST: "What I *said* was: There's a coven of witches operating in the White House. We all know that. Look at the bags under Bill Clinton's eyes. The man can't get any sleep. All that chanting, the burning incense, the Doors albums wailing constantly... *Someone* is organizing these people."

CALLER: "And Zoe Baird? Was she a..."

HOST: "The jury's still out on that one, Betty, although there *was* a makeshift altar in the back of her house, with chicken feathers and the bones of small animals scattered about. Draw your own conclusions."

CALLER: "I find your program very informative."

HOST: "Rich from White Marsh."

CALLER: "Marty, I see Congress is thinking about voting itself a big, fat pay raise again."

HOST: "I read that, too."

CALLER: "Amazing. Here these people are part of a known baby-selling ring and the..."

HOST: "I'm sorry — a *what* ring?"

CALLER: "Congress is running a baby-selling ring, Marty. My niece worked as a page there one summer. She said the average Caucasian baby was going for upwards of $10,000. They use the money to pay for a big party at the end of the year."

HOST: "A party?"

CALLER: "Kegs of beer, male and female strippers, roulette wheels..."

HOST: "Let me get this straight..."

CALLER: "Teddy Kennedy runs the whole show."

HOST: "Why doesn't *that* surprise me? This guy must have tiny horns growing out the top of his head."

CALLER: "Everyone calls him 'The Broker.' He has catalogs on the coffee table in his office filled with pictures of babies for sale."

HOST: "Daniel Webster just rolled over in his grave. Let's go to Rich on his car phone."

CALLER: "Marty, this business about gays in the military. I was in 'Nam in '67 and we had several gays in our platoon. By the time of the Tet Offensive, they were demanding to wear pink nighties into battle."

HOST: "Thank God MacArthur isn't alive to hear this."

CALLER: "Don't get me wrong, they were good soldiers. But you couldn't wear pink in the jungle. The Viet Cong spotters were picking us up from miles away."

HOST: "Frank from Randallstown, you're on the air."

CALLER: "Marty, I hear a London tabloid has pictures of Clinton taken in Hanoi in '67. One shows Clinton with one arm around Ho Chi Minh."

HOST: "Let's go to Rose in Essex."

CALLER: "Yeah, hi, Marty. That poll you took on what form of capital punishment people favored? Is it too late to get in on that?"

HOST: "Nope. What's your pleasure?"

CALLER: "Put me down for hacking and dismembering."

HOST *(sound of paper shuffling)*: "Y'know, it's funny. I thought a lot more people would go for being bound and dragged through scrub brush behind a Jeep Cherokee."

CALLER: "Marty, can I say one more thing? At first I thought it was sickening the way people were jumping on President Clinton. But that business about Hillary being a witch...I'm sorry, we just can't have that."

HOST: "Amen... Back after these messages."

A reinvented image for Miami

After a ninth foreign tourist was slain recently in Florida, the Greater Miami Convention and Visitors Bureau last week did what needed to be done. It hired a public relations firm. — Washington Post.

To: Greater Miami CVB
From: Richard O. Pillo and Associates
Re: Reshaping the image of South Florida

First, many thanks for retaining our firm. Our goal now is to counter the negative image of Miami as, to use your words, the "Dodge City of the Tropics."

Frankly, our task won't be easy. As you know, we were retained by the city of New York in the wake of the World Trade Center bombing. Our ad campaign ("New York — Our *Other* Tall Buildings Aren't Charred!") proved only modestly successful, and fear, like the smell of nitroglycerin, lingers still in the Big Apple.

Tourism figures remain low; and, sadly, too many fussy travelers are allowing exorbitant hotel and restaurant prices and a few hundred thousand muggers, hookers and crack dealers to influence their vacation plans.

Nevertheless, we've developed a bold, three-tiered approach to solving Miami's problems:

Step 1: We propose a series of TV commercials built around the slogan: "Miami — It's Not *That* Bad!"

These commercials would focus on your city's natural beauty and aquatic charm, interspersed with shots of smiling, waving Miamians, many of them unarmed. *(If enough citizens can't be found without side holsters or the tell-tale sweatshirt bulge that signals a 9 mm in a waistband, perhaps some of the filming could be done in San Diego or Tucson.)*

With these spots, we hope to convey the message that, although Miami is often portrayed as a festering wasteland plagued by drug wars and psychotic hoodlums, it's also home to dozens of decent people *not* connected to the narcotics trade.

In other words: "Don't be a baby! C'mon down, the weather's great!"

Step 2: We hope to introduce an intensive ad campaign specifically designed to attract foreign tourists from such "trouble spots" as Bosnia, Angola, Sri Lanka, Northern Ireland, etc.

Our thinking is: Compared to the violence the people of these countries have experienced, Miami will seem positively tranquil and idyllic.

We daresay that if a hardy group of, oh, Bosnian Muslims were standing outside the Miami Sheraton and one of its members was gunned down in a senseless drive-by shooting, the thinking would be: "Well, we lost Georgi, but that's no reason not to take in Sea World this afternoon as originally planned."

As another example, if a delegation of Belfast IRA regulars were set upon by pistol-packing thugs inside Joe Robbie Stadium, the IRA force would no doubt pull out their own weapons, squeeze off a few rounds and go back to watching the ballgame.

Let's face it, this is the type of tourist Miami wants to attract: bold, adventurous folks, not squeamish about small-arms fire. People who won't stay holed up in their hotel rooms wailing and wringing their hands each and every time someone close to them is shot, but who will be out in the bars, restaurants and theaters *spending money*.

Step 3: At Pillo and Associates, we believe in turning negatives into positives whenever possible.

Instead of bemoaning the crime-wave washing over your fair city, why not put it to good use?

Let the armies of the world know that Miami's streets could serve as an excellent training site for urban guerrilla warfare. Recently, U.S. armed forces were engaged in bitter house-to-house fighting in Mogadishu, Somalia. Wouldn't the presence of 10,000 or so troops in Miami a few months earlier have boosted the economy while also providing our soldiers an ideal training ground?

But don't stop there. Invite combat doctors and nurses to come here to study the gaping wounds caused by the modern weaponry carried by Miami's criminals.

And schedule conventions designed to attract "Soldiers of Fortune," organized crime cartels, leftist insurrectionists, etc.

Soon, Miami would be a truly exciting city, teeming with thousands of drunken, free-spending soldiers and sailors, survivalist kooks, cults, mercenaries, international terrorists and ne'er-do-wells.

Instead of whining about the PR "black eye" Miami has suffered, we urge you, to puff up your chests and shout: "Yes, this *is* a dangerous city. We welcome your business!"

"Miami: Come See Us — If You Have The Guts!"

Has a nice ring to it, eh?

Mosquitoes ride again

The mosquitoes rumbled into the back yard on their little Harleys, scaring the hell out of the children and not doing much for my state of mind, either.

"Whatcha doing?" they growled.

We were having a little cook-out, I explained.

Nothing fancy, I said, just some hot dogs and hamburgers. Maybe potato salad, too, and a few nice garden tomatoes that we...

"SHUT UP!" interrupted the head mosquito, the swarthy one with the bandoliers across his chest. "I'll do the talking around here."

We don't want any trouble, I said. Why don't you boys mosey on back to whatever stinking gutter or fetid swamp you came from. That way nobody will get hurt.

The mosquitoes just laughed and revved their motorcycles even louder.

I got the impression they planned to stick around for a while, judging by the tiny bibs they were putting on and the hungry way they eyed me.

I'd seen that look before, a look that says: "Mister, you're just another meal to me. I'll eat you or I'll chow down on a pile of week-old garbage. It don't matter to me."

Sure enough, things got ugly in a hurry with these mosquitoes.

Oh, they didn't kick over the picnic table or throw any liquor bottles through the picture window or try to dance with anyone's wife.

But they ruined the cook-out just the same.

Lord knows we tried to carry on as if they weren't there, but pretty soon we were all cursing and slapping at our arms and legs.

Twenty minutes later, we retreated into the house and spent the rest of the evening listening to them carry on in the yard, hooting and hollering, cracking beers and setting off cherry bombs and doing wheelies around the trash can.

Scientists blame the record number of mosquitoes on all the rain we've had recently, which certainly makes sense; my back yard has looked like Lake Superior this year.

All I know is the mosquitoes at my place are as big as bats.

In fact, I thought they *were* bats at first, but then I remembered that bats don't show up until it gets dark, whereas these mosquitoes will join you for breakfast with twelve pieces of American Tourister luggage, making it fairly clear they plan to stay a while.

And these mosquitoes are as brazen as the devil, too.

The other day I was sitting outside reading when a whole bunch of them swaggered up without so much as an "Excuse me."

And believe me, they weren't there to ask directions to the nearest mud puddle. They were there to hassle me, pure and simple.

So I whipped out a can of "Off," which is the Rolls Royce of mosquito repellents, or so I'm told.

They say that if you spray this stuff on your arms and legs in front of a mosquito, it's the equivalent of waving a silver crucifix in front of a vampire.

In other words, for your troubles to be over, you don't have to lock yourself in a closet until sun-up.

"Stay away!" I said, waving the "Off" in the air. "Don't make me use it! I swear, one more step and someone's gonna get hurt!"

But these mosquitoes didn't bat an eyelash.

If anything, it made them even more mouthy and sarcastic.

"Oooooooh! He's got 'Off'!" they said. "We're so-o-o scared! Look, we're sha-a-aking!"

With that, they all laughed and slapped each other on the back. Then they went off to tap the beer keg they had dragged into the tall grass, and pretty soon they had the stereo cranking out "Louie, Louie."

At first, I went back to my book and tried to ignore them.

But it's pretty hard to concentrate on plot structure and character development when you're slapping your neck and losing the kind of blood normally associated with a gunshot wound.

I'm no doctor, but I gotta be dropping two, three pints of blood per chapter — mosquito repellent or *no* mosquito repellent.

They say the average adult has about six quarts of blood in his body, but you couldn't prove it by me. Not with this mosquito Woodstock taking place in my backyard.

In fact, the next time the Red Cross asks for blood, I'll have to turn them down. They can get in line behind the mosquitoes.

Though, unlike the Red Cross, the mosquitoes don't exactly hook up IV lines and hand out juice and cookies when it's over.

You're lucky to get five minutes of peace, never mind a "Thank you."

A dog's life is not carefree

Does your dog hate to see you leave? Does your dog cry, urinate, defecate, or destroy the house when home alone? If so, s/he may be suffering from separation anxiety and be eligible to participate in a major pharmaceutical company-sponsored study. — Classified ad in New York newspaper

Don't go, Phil, is what I said. He was in the foyer reaching for his briefcase and that *goofy* hat he wears when it's raining. Phil, I said, every time you leave it just tears me up and I... I *worry* about you so much.

This is what I told him, only it came out "Woof, woof, woof" like it always does and Phil just stared at me with that clueless look on his face. He might be the dumbest human being I've ever seen.

"Coco, get out of the way," he said. "I'm late for work."

Which is when I caused that big scene. I started jumping up on him and scratching at his raincoat and yelling: "Phil, please, take me with you. I'll be good, I swear. You won't hear a peep out of me at the office. *Please*, Phil, please! I'm begging you!"

I don't know... I try to speak slowly and to articulate, but it always comes out "Woof, woof, woof," which they don't get and which annoys them after a while. Sometimes, they even tell you to shut up.

This time Phil pushed me aside with his leg and squeezed out the door. Then he slammed the door in my face, and I was left with that awful silence.

Apparently, at that point, I just went berserk.

All I remember is scratching frantically at the door and yelling: "Phil, Phil, come back!"

Then I jumped on the couch by the window and watched him climb into the Buick, and then I ran back to the door and began scratching, scratching, scratching again.

I thought I was going crazy. I was barking and barking and pretty soon there was this loud ringing in my ears, which, thank God, turned out to be the phone.

Then I started running around in circles. I thought I was losing it. I really did.

Anyway, all that happened this morning.

Now I'm just sitting here on the couch, staring out the window and waiting for Phil to come home.

The boredom is what kills you. You get up in the morning and he walks you and feeds you. Then he leaves for work and you think: Now what?

Sleep a little, stare out the window, chew the hell out of the rattan chair downstairs — that's basically all I do all day. It's not much of a life.

Every once in a while, the UPS guy pulls up in his truck to drop off a package and I'll start barking like a nut and hurling myself at the door.

But it's all an act. Tell you the truth, I wish the guy would come in. I could use the company.

That reminds me of the time I was about a year-old. Phil, who was leaving for work, said: "Take care of the house, Coco, and don't let any strangers in."

And I'm like: *What?* You gotta be kidding me, Phil. I'm a *cocker spaniel*, for crying out loud! I see some guy climbing through the window with a ski mask and a gun, I'm heading the other way, pronto. Hey, I'm not about to take a bullet for anyone in *this* house, Jack.

In fact, as he was leaving that day, I said: "Phil, you're so worried about security, get yourself a Rottweiler or a German shepherd, one of those big, aggressive mutts."

But for the 400th time it came out "Woof, woof, woof" and Phil just gave me a pat on the head and walked out the door.

The thing is, I don't know which is worse sometimes: being alone or having Phil around the house.

The other day, he says: "C'mon, Coco. Let's go out in the backyard."

Right away I'm thinking: Phil, are we gonna play that stupid game where you throw the tennis ball and I gotta run after it and bring it back?

In the first place, God knows where that tennis ball has been. Plus, I end up getting all that fuzz from the ball in my mouth and it tastes awful. Makes you gag, is what it does.

But for some reason, Phil gets a big kick out of seeing me run around like a lunatic after this ball and then collapse from exhaustion.

What was that?! Was that a car door? Is Phil home? Boy, he's really gonna be steamed when he sees that rattan chair.

I can see the look on his... aw, it's not him. It's the next-door neighbor.

Where *is* Phil, anyway. He *said* he'd be home by six.

U.S. is going to the dogs

As if anyone needs further proof that the country is going to hell in a handbasket, I offer up something observed the other day in a department store.

There's no need to mention the name of the store here, as this isn't meant to cause any undue embarrassment.

Plus, they might sue me. Although to tell you the truth, after what I saw in their store, *I'm* the one who should be hiring a lawyer. You talk about emotional strain.

Anyway, I'm walking along in this store when... did I mention the store is part of a chain? A *well-known* national chain? I should mention that. The name begins with the letter C. That's as far as I'll go.

OK, the name ends in R. No, that's it. My lips are sealed.

So I'm walking along in this store when suddenly I spot a rack of sun visors.

There are red visors and blue visors and yellow visors, all decorated with tiny... chili peppers. I know that's sort of hard to visualize. The whole look was kind of Andy Warholish in a Tex-Mex sort of way.

So I stop to check out the visors, thinking I might pick up a couple for the kids and thereby enhance my already lofty status in their eyes.

Then I see something that makes my blood run cold.

Stapled to the product is a rather crude cardboard sign that says: "Pet Visor."

And underneath is a picture of some stupid-looking mutt wearing this visor — which, it goes without saying, makes the animal appear even more stupid-looking.

God in heaven! So it's come to this, I thought.

It has actually come to the point in this country where we are now worrying about whether or not a dog is squinting into the sun.

Makes you proud to be an American, huh? The Japanese are manufacturing sophisticated computers the size of your fingernail. The Germans are making incredible strides in biotechnology.

And we're turning out doggie visors — when we're not worrying about whether to put the young Elvis or the Lounge Lizard Elvis on a stamp.

As you can imagine, the whole incident with the visors left me in quite a state, to the point where I had to go directly home and lie down in a dark room for several hours.

Then, that evening, a related incident confirmed that we are in the midst of a long, slow decline back into the morass.

An acquaintance of ours dropped by after dinner. Normally a gregarious woman, she appeared to be upset about something.

At last we managed to pry it out of her. She was worried about her dog.

"Your *dog?*" I said. "What happened? Is he sick? Was he hit by a car?"

"No, no," she said. "Although this is just as bad. He lost his rubber bone."

"He lost his... WHAT?"

Well, from what I could piece together, the dog had some sort of rubber bone toy that he was particularly fond of.

Apparently he would play with this thing for hours. But the toy disappeared two days ago from the backyard. And now the dog seemed to be taking it very hard.

"All he does is lie around and mope," she said.

I'm telling you, it was all I could do not to reach over and cuff this woman alongside the head.

"Look," I said, "it seems to me you have two options here. Number one, you buy the mutt another rubber bone and hope he starts wagging his tail again and lives happily ever after.

"Or number two — and this is the option I favor — you grab the dog by his collar, get right in his face and scream: 'SNAP OUT OF IT, DAMMIT. THE BONE'S GONE! NOW GO PLAY WITH THAT TENNIS BALL!'"

The woman flinched. An unhealthy silence descended on the room for several moments.

"You don't *like* dogs, do you?" she said at last.

"On the contrary," I said. "I *love* dogs."

There have been dogs in my family ever since I was five. I had a 160-pound St. Bernard for three years, which is sort of like living with a Shetland pony.

"But here's the thing," I said. "I try not to forget that they're *dogs. THEY'RE NOT PEOPLE!*"

"Which means I don't dress them up in sweaters, like some of these nuts do.

"I don't put little booties on their paws. I don't buy sun visors for their little eyes. I don't feed them $40 cuts of meat.

"And if they get, ahem, *upset* over a missing toy, I have a little chat with them. To, you know, cheer 'em up again."

The woman was quiet for a moment.

They she brightened and said: "They have *sun visors* for dogs?!"

You could almost hear the cash register ring.